BIG CATS
& WILD DOGS

Rhonda Klevansky and Jen Green

Consultants

Dr Nigel Dunstone and Douglas Richardson

southwater

This edition is published by Southwater

Southwater is an imprint of Anness Publishing Ltd
Hermes House, 88–89 Blackfriars Road, London SE1 8HA
tel. 020 7401 2077; fax 020 7633 9499
www.southwaterbooks.com; info@anness.com

UK agent: The Manning Partnership Ltd, 6 The Old Dairy, Melcombe
Road, Bath BA2 3LR; tel. 01225 478444; fax 01225 478440;
sales@manning-partnership.co.uk

UK distributor: Grantham Book Services Ltd, Isaac Newton Way, Alma
Park Industrial Estate, Grantham, Lincs NG31 9SD; tel. 01476
541080; fax 01476 541061; orders@gbs.tbs-ltd.co.uk

North American agent/distributor: National Book Network, 4501
Forbes Boulevard, Suite 200, Lanham, MD 20706; tel. 301 459 3366;
fax 301 429 5746; www.nbnbooks.com

Australian agent/distributor: Pan Macmillan Australia, Level 18, St
Martins Tower, 31 Market St, Sydney, NSW 2000; tel. 1300 135 113;
fax 1300 135 103; customer.service@macmillan.com.au

New Zealand agent/distributor: David Bateman Ltd, 30 Tarndale Grove,
Off Bush Road, Albany, Auckland; tel. (09) 415 7664; fax (09) 415 8892

A CIP catalogue record for this book
is available from the British Library.

Publisher: Joanna Lorenz
Managing Editor: Gilly Cameron
Cooper
Project Editors: Charlotte Hurdman,
Nicole Pearson and Molly Perham
Designers:Traffika Publishing Ltd;
Ann Samuel
Illustrators: David Webb, Vanessa
Card, Peter Bull, Sarah Smith
Picture Researchers:
Elizabeth Walsh, Kay Rowley,
Cathy Stastney
Production Controller:
Darren Price

Previously published in two separate
volumes, *Nature Watch: Big Cats* and
Nature Watch: Wolves

10 9 8 7 6 5 4 3 2 1

CONTENTS

4 Introduction

6 THE WORLD OF BIG CATS

INTRODUCING BIG CATS
8 What is a Cat?
10 The Big Cats

HOW BIG CATS WORK
12 Bones and Teeth
14 Muscles and Claws
16 Sight and Sound
18 Touching, Tasting and Smelling
20 Spots and Stripes
22 On the Move
24 Focus on the Hunting Cheetah
26 Communication

CATCHING PREY
28 Hunting Prey
30 Killing Prey
32 Focus on the Lone Leopard

HOW BIG CATS BEHAVE
34 Living Together
36 Focus on a Pride
38 Finding a Mate
40 Giving Birth
42 Focus on Cute Cubs
44 Growing Up
46 Enemies of Big Cats

WHERE BIG CATS LIVE
48 Mountain Cats
50 Forest Dwellers
52 Focus on Siberian Tigers
54 On the Savanna
56 Desert Cats

FACTS ABOUT BIG CATS
58 Killer Cats
60 Cats in Danger
62 Protecting Cats

64 THE WORLD OF WILD DOGS

INTRODUCING WILD DOGS
66 What is a Wolf?
68 The Wolf Family
70 Wild Dogs
72 Focus on Domestic Dogs

HOW WILD DOGS WORK
74 Body Shapes
76 Body Parts
78 On the Move
80 Fur Coats
82 Sight and Sound
84 Smell, Touch
   and Taste

WILD DOG BEHAVIOR
86 Living Together
88 Focus on a
   Wolf Pack
90 Home Territory
92 A Meaty Diet

94 Going Hunting
96 Focus on African Hunting Dogs

LIFE CYCLES
98 Finding a Mate
100 Newborn Cubs
102 Growing Up

WHERE WILD DOGS LIVE
104 Icy Wastes
106 In the Forest
108 Grassland and Desert
110 Focus on Coyotes

FACTS ABOUT WILD DOGS
112 Relatives and Namesakes
114 Focus on Foxes
116 Fact or Fiction?
118 Natural Enemies
120 Wild Dogs and People
122 Conservation

124 Glossary
127 Index

INTRODUCTION

If you have a pet cat, you will be familiar with the way it hunts for prey such as mice and birds, how it grooms itself and how it protects its territory from other cats. Big wild cats are larger versions of domestic cats, and behave in much the same way. Fossil records of cats similar to modern wild cats date back about 10 million years. Wolves date back at least two million years, and wild dogs and, later, pet dogs evolved from these early wolves. The first domestic dogs were probably bred from wolves tamed by hunters.

Big cats, wild dogs and wolves are carnivorous (meat-eating) mammals, of which there are several distinct families. Cats all belong to the family Felidae, and there are 38 different species of wild cat, big and small. Wild dogs and wolves belong to the family Canidae, which has 37 species. Both families are native to every continent except Australia and Antarctica.

One of the characteristics that cats, dogs and wolves have in common is their teeth—strong back teeth called carnassials, pointed canines, sharp incisors and scissor-like molars. With these fearsome weapons they can tear, pierce, cut, and chew the flesh of their prey. Another common feature is their fur, which preserves their body heat.

Big cats are the most specialized of the carnivores, and are well adapted to a hunting life. As well as their specially designed teeth, their ears, eyes, whiskers and nose are well-developed sense organs. In order to pursue prey, big cats make use of scent, sight, and even clues such as footmarks. They are masters in the art of leaping: from a running, walking, standing or sitting position they can catapult into the air to hit their prey with stunning impact. They land with jaws wide open, teeth bared, and claws extended ready to sink into the throat and flesh of their

RED FOX

The red fox is most active just after dusk and before dawn. It is most conspicuous during the mating season in late winter and can be recognized by its calls: the male fox has a sharp bark, but the female's scream is very distinctive. Red foxes spend most of the day curled up in their burrow, called an "earth."

LION

The male lion has a tawny mane which darkens with age. Old males are often known as "black-maned" lions. The mane makes the male appear larger than he really is, helping to attract females and frighten off rival males.

prey. Cats have the sharpest claws of all mammals, claws that can be withdrawn into a sheath by all species except the cheetah. In this way, the claws are protected and the cat can stalk prey silently on its pads.

Wild dogs and wolves all have elongated jaws with more than forty teeth. The canines are especially long and dagger-like for holding on to prey, and in some species the molars are used for grinding bones. Unlike cats, they cannot retract their claws. Wild dogs can swim, and a few can climb trees, although they are adapted to life on the ground. Their sense of smell is exceptionally well developed and this, with their good eyesight and keen hearing, allows them to follow a trail through a forest on a dark night.

Most carnivores tend only to take prey that are about their own size or smaller, but some, such as lions, can kill much larger animals. Others may band together in packs to overpower larger prey. The big cats usually kill their prey by suffocation; the smaller carnivores tend to have a killing bite; but many, such as the wolf and the hyena, kill by tearing their prey to pieces.

In many parts of the world big cats, wild dogs and wolves are in danger of extinction. They have either been hunted for their skins, teeth, bones, and other body parts; or by local farmers because they fear the animals will kill livestock. In recent years conservationists have set up reserves and protected areas where these splendid animals can live without human interference.

WOLF

The grey wolf is fiercely territorial—it scent-marks boundaries and makes its presence known to other wolf packs by howling. Similarly, rival packs may answer the calls with those of their own. A wolf that has been driven from the pack, or has left of its own accord, is called a lone wolf. It avoids contact with packs and rarely howls.

LEOPARD

Young leopards stay with their mother for about two years, learning how to hunt and fend for themselves. Leopards are excellent climbers and spend much of their time up in trees. They may lie in silent ambush on a branch, or carry their kill up into a tree to store it beyond the reach of scavengers such as lions, hyenas, and jackals.

The leopard's strongly contrasting markings break up the outline of its body and help it to blend into the bark of a tree.

CARACAL

The caracal's most startling feature is the long tufts on its ears. These may help it locate prey. The caracal is related to both the leopard and the lynx. It lives in grasslands, open woodland and scrub in Africa and parts of Asia.

THE WORLD OF BIG CATS

The largest and most powerful of the big cats are the tiger and the lion, which are capable of killing animals more than twice their own size. Leopards and cheetahs are known for their swiftness, sprinting at high speed after their prey. The jaguar is an agile tree-climber, lying in wait on the branch of a tree. Nature's most terrifying predators, all the big cats inspire in us both fear and awe.

What is a Cat?

Cats are native to every continent except Australia and Antarctica. All cats are mammals with fine fur that is often beautifully marked. They are skilled hunters and killers with strong agile bodies, acute senses and sharp teeth and claws. Cats are stealthy and intelligent animals, and many are solitary and very mysterious. Although cats vary in size from the domestic (house) cat to the huge Siberian tiger, they all belong to the same family, the Felidae. This means that both wild and domestic cats look alike and behave in very similar ways. In all, there are 38 different species of cat.

▲ **LONG TAIL**
A cat's long tail helps it balance as it runs. Cats also use their tails to signal their feelings to other cats.

All cats have short, rounded heads.

Whiskers help a cat feel its surroundings.

The body of a cat is muscular and supple, with a broad, powerful chest.

▲ **BIG BITE**
As this tiger yawns it reveals its sharp teeth and strong jaws that can give a lethal bite. Cats use their long, curved canine teeth for killing prey.

▲ **BIG CATS**
Cats are very specialized meat-eaters. They are the perfect carnivore, with excellent hearing and eyesight. Their curved, razor-sharp claws, used for catching and holding prey, are retractable. This means they can be pulled into the paws to protect them when running. The hair covering a cat's paws and surrounding the pads helps it move silently.

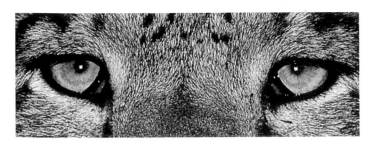

▲ NIGHT SIGHT

The pupils (dark centers) of cats' eyes close to a slit or small circle during the day to keep out the glare. At night they open up to let in as much light as possible. This enables a cat to see at night as well as during the day.

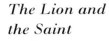

The Lion and the Saint

St. Jerome was a Christian scholar who lived from about A.D. 331 to 420. According to legend, he found an injured lion in the desert with a thorn in its paw. Instead of attacking him, the lion befriended the saint when he removed the thorn. St. Jerome is often shown with a lion sitting at his feet.

Very soft fur is kept clean by regular grooming with the tongue and paws.

A long tail helps the cat balance when it runs and leaps on prey.

Did you know? Some Arctic cultures believe that cats represent the spirits of the dead.

Cats walk on their toes, not on the whole foot.

Large ears draw in sounds.

CATS' EARS ▶

A cat's ears are set high on its head. This gives a keen hunter the best possible chance of picking up sounds. The ears have a rounded shape, which enables sounds to be picked up from many directions. Cats can also rotate their ears to face the source of a sound.

The Big Cats

Scientists classify (arrange) the members of the cat family into related groups. The two main groups are small cats (the domestic cat and many wild cats) and the big cats (the tiger, lion, leopard, snow leopard and jaguar). The clouded leopard and the cheetah are each grouped separately, but many people regard them as big cats. Big cats differ from small cats not only because of their size. Big cats can roar, but small cats cannot. Small cats purr. They have a special bone, the hyoid, at the base of their tongues that enables them to breathe and purr at the same time. Big cats have elastic cartilage instead and can only purr when they breathe out. The puma is in fact a very large small cat. It is discussed here because of its size.

▲ **LION**
The lion is the only social cat and lives in a family group called a pride. Adult male lions, unlike other big cats, have a long, thick mane of hair. Female lions do not have manes.

▲ **PUMA**
The puma is also called the cougar or mountain lion. Although it is about the same size as a leopard, a puma is considered a small cat because it can purr. Pumas live in North and South America.

◄ **CHEETAH**
The tall cheetah is built like a slim athlete and is able to chase prey at great speed. Cheetahs are different from other cats in that they have retractable claws, but no sheaths to cover them. It was once thought that cheetahs were related to dogs, but scientists now think that their closest cousins are pumas.

LEOPARD

The leopard is built for bursts of speed and for climbing trees. Heavier than a cheetah, this cat is not as large and bulky as a tiger or a lion. Its spotted coat helps to hide the cat as it hunts in wooded grassland. Black leopards are called panthers. They are the same species, but their spots are hidden.

SNOW LEOPARD

Snow leopards are a different species from true leopards. These rare cats have very thick coats to keep them warm in the high mountains of central Asia. They have very long tails, which help them to balance as they leap from rock to rock in their mountainous surroundings.

JAGUAR

The jaguar is sometimes confused with a leopard, but it is stockier and not as agile. It lives throughout South America in forested habitats where it needs strength to climb rather than speed to run.

TIGER

The most powerful and largest of all the big cats is the tiger. A tiger reaches on average a length of over 6½ feet and weighs about 500 pounds. The biggest tigers live in the snowy forests of Siberia in Russia. A few tigers also live in tropical forest reserves and swamps in Asia.

Did you know? Although lions are called the King of the Jungle, they do not live there.

Bones and Teeth

The skeleton of a cat gives it its shape and has 230 bones (a human has about 206). Its short and round skull is joined to the spine (backbone), which supports the body. Vertebrae (bones of the spine) protect the spinal cord, which is the main nerve cable in the body. The ribs are joined to the spine, forming a cage that protects a cat's heart and lungs. Cats' teeth are designed for tearing and chewing meat. Wild cats have to be very careful not to damage their teeth, because with broken teeth they would quickly die from starvation.

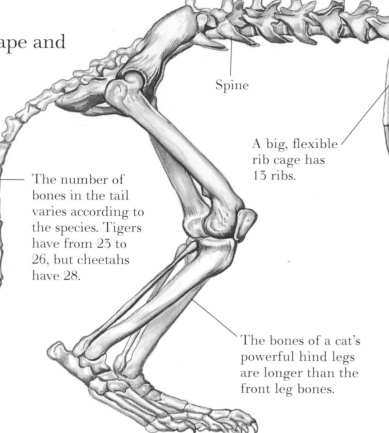

Spine

A big, flexible rib cage has 13 ribs.

The number of bones in the tail varies according to the species. Tigers have from 23 to 26, but cheetahs have 28.

The bones of a cat's powerful hind legs are longer than the front leg bones.

▲ **THE FRAME**
The powerfully built skeleton of a tiger is similar to all cats' skeletons. Cats have short necks with seven compressed vertebrae. These help to streamline and balance the cat so that it can achieve greater speeds. All cats have slightly different shoulder bones. A cheetah has long shoulder bones to which sprinting muscles are attached. A leopard, however, has short shoulder bones and thicker, tree-climbing muscles.

◄ **CANINES AND CARNASSIALS**
A tiger reveals its fearsome teeth. Its long, curved canines are adapted to fit between the neck bones of its prey to break the spinal cord. Like all carnivores, cats have strong back teeth, called carnassials. These do most of the cutting by tearing off pieces of meat.

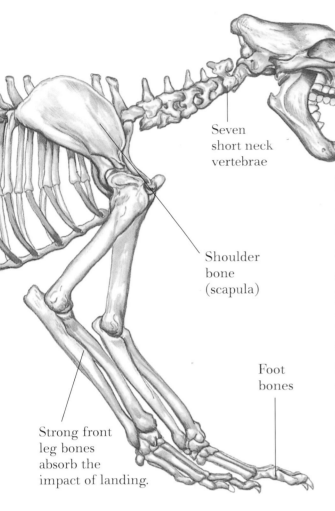

Seven short neck vertebrae

Shoulder bone (scapula)

Foot bones

Strong front leg bones absorb the impact of landing.

LANDING FEET ▶

As it falls, this cat twists its supple, flexible spine to make sure its feet will be in the right place for landing. Cats almost always land on their feet when they fall. This helps them to avoid injury as they leap on prey or jump from a tree.

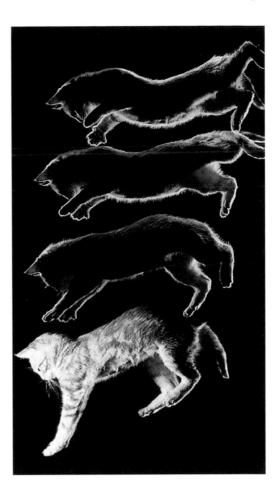

▼ CHEWING ON A BONE

Ravenous lions feast on the carcass of their latest kill. Cats' jaws are hinged so that their jaw bones can move only from side to side, not up and down. Because of this, cats eat on one side of their mouths at a time and often tilt their heads when they eat.

▼ CAT SKULL

Like all cats' skulls, this tiger's skull has a high crown at the back giving lots of space for its strong neck muscles. Big eye sockets allow it to see well to the sides as well as to the front. Its short jaws can open wide to deliver a powerful bite.

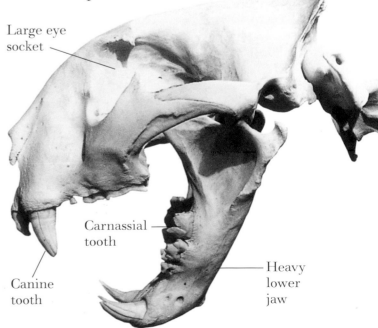

Large eye socket

Carnassial tooth

Canine tooth

Heavy lower jaw

13

Muscles and Claws

Both inside and out, cats are designed to be skilled hunters and killers. Thick back and shoulder muscles help them to be excellent jumpers and climbers. Sharp, curved claws that grow from all of their digits (toes) are their weapons. One of the digits on a cat's front foot is called the dew claw. This is held off the ground to keep it sharp and ready to hold prey. Cats are warm-blooded, which means that their bodies stay at the same temperature no matter how hot or cold the weather is. The fur on their skin keeps them warm when conditions are cold. When it is hot, cats cool down by sweating through their noses and paw pads.

Heracles and the Nemean Lion
The mythical Greek hero Heracles was the son of the god Zeus and tremendously strong. As a young man he committed a terrible crime. Part of his punishment was to kill the Nemean lion. The lion had impenetrable skin and could not be killed with arrows or spears. Heracles chased the lion into a cave and strangled it with his hands. He wore its skin as a shield and its head as a helmet.

▼ KNOCKOUT CLAWS

Cheetahs have well-developed dew claws that stick out from their front legs. They use these claws to knock down prey before grabbing its throat or muzzle to strangle it. Other cats use their dew claws to grip while climbing or to hold onto prey. Cats have five claws, including the dew claw, on their front paws. On their back paws, they have only four claws.

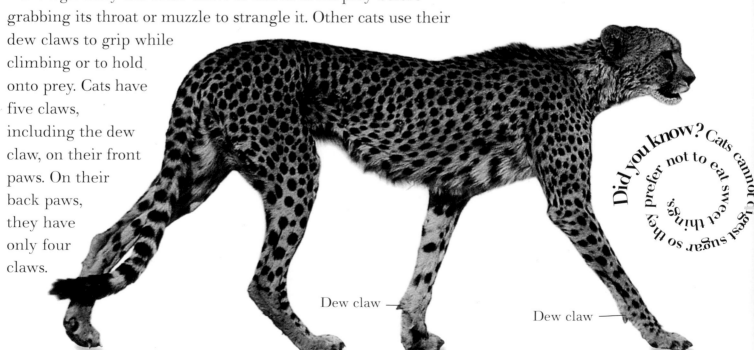

Dew claw

Dew claw

Did you know? Cats cannot taste sugar so they prefer not to eat sweet things.

14

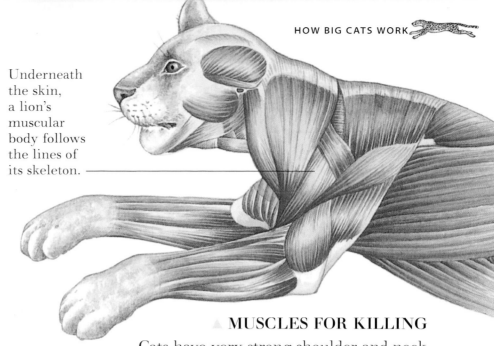

Underneath the skin, a lion's muscular body follows the lines of its skeleton.

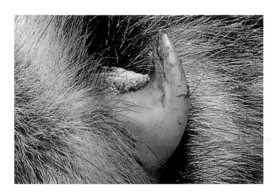

▲ TIGER CLAW

This is the extended claw of a tiger. Cats' claws are made of keratin, just like human fingernails. They need to be kept sharp all the time.

▲ MUSCLES FOR KILLING

Cats have very strong shoulder and neck muscles for attacking prey. The muscles also absorb some of the impact when the cat pounces.

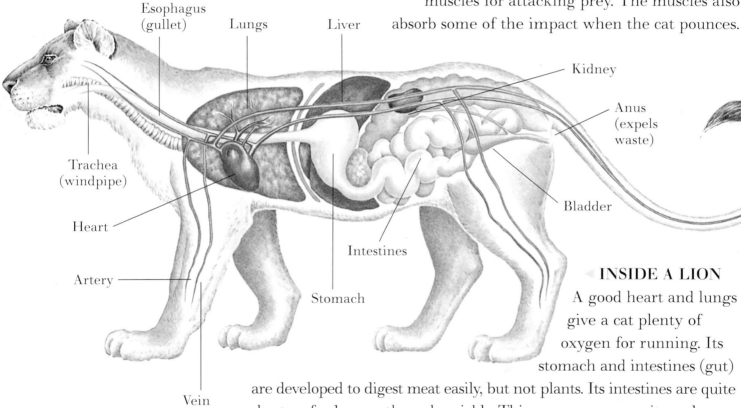

Esophagus (gullet)

Lungs

Liver

Kidney

Anus (expels waste)

Trachea (windpipe)

Heart

Artery

Vein

Stomach

Intestines

Bladder

◄ INSIDE A LION

A good heart and lungs give a cat plenty of oxygen for running. Its stomach and intestines (gut) are developed to digest meat easily, but not plants. Its intestines are quite short, so food passes through quickly. This means as soon as it needs more food, a cat is light enough to run and pounce. However, once a lion has had a big meal, it does not need to eat again for several days.

CLAW PROTECTION ►

Cats retract (pull back) their claws into fleshy sheaths to protect them. This prevents them from getting blunt or damaged. Only cheetahs do not have sheaths.

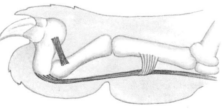

Sheathed claw is protected by a fleshy covering.

Flexed muscle

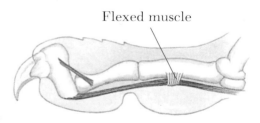

The claw is unsheathed when a muscle tightens.

Sight and Sound

To hunt well and not be seen or heard by prey or enemies, cats use their senses of sight, sound and touch. Cats' eyesight is excellent. Their eyes are adapted for night vision, but they can also see well in the day. Cats' eyes are big compared to the size of their heads. They have good binocular vision, which allows them to accurately judge how far away objects are. At night, cats see in black and white. They can see colors in the day, but not as well as humans can. Cats have very good hearing, much better than a human's. They can hear small animals rustling through the grass or even moving around in their burrows underground.

Did you know? A cat's pupils open wide when it is frightened and close up when it is angry.

▲ **CAUGHT IN BRIGHT LIGHT**
Cats' eyes are very sensitive to light. During the day in bright light, the pupils of the eyes close right down, letting in only as much light as is needed to see well. A domestic cat's pupils close down to slits, while most big cats' pupils close to tiny circles.

◄ **GLOWING EYES**
Behind the retinas (light-sensitive areas) in this leopard's eyes is a reflecting layer called the tapetum lucidum. This helps to absorb extra light in the dark. When light shines into the eyes at night, the reflectors glow.

PREY IN SIGHT ▶

As it stalks through the long grass a lion must pounce at just the right moment if it is to catch its prey. Binocular vision helps the cat to judge when to strike. Because its eyes are set slightly apart at the front of the head, their field of view overlaps. This enables a cat to judge the position of its prey exactly.

▲ ROUND-EYED

This puma's rounded pupils have closed down in daylight. In dim light, the pupils will expand wide to let in as much light as possible.

SHARP EARS ▶

Cats' ears are designed for them to hear very well. This Siberian lynx lives in snowy forests where the sound is often muffled. It has specially-shaped, big ears to catch as much sound as possible.

Large earflaps concentrate sound waves deep into each ear.

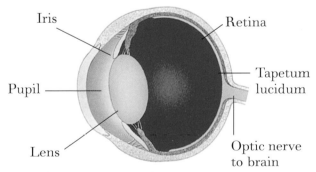

Iris

Retina

Pupil

Tapetum lucidum

Lens

Optic nerve to brain

▲ INSIDE THE EYE

The lens focuses light rays to produce a sharp image on the retina. Impulses from the retina are carried to the brain by the optic nerve. Cats have a membrane that can be pulled over the surface of the eye to keep out dirt and dust.

Touching, Tasting and Smelling

Like all animals, cats feel things with nerves in their skin, but they have another important touching tool—whiskers. These long, stiff hairs on the face have very sensitive nerve endings at their roots. Some whiskers are for protection. Anything brushing against the whiskers above a cat's eyes will make it blink. Cats use smell and taste to communicate with each other. A cat's tongue is a useful tool and its nose is very sensitive. Thin, curled bones in the nose carry scents inward to smell receptors. Unlike most animals, cats have special places on the roofs of their mouths to distinguish scents, especially of other cats.

▲ **TONGUE TOOL**
A leopard curls the tip of its tongue like a spoon to lap up water. After several laps it will drink the water in one gulp. As well as drinking, the tongue is used for tasting, scraping meat off a carcass and grooming.

◀ **ROUGH TONGUE**
A tiger's bright pink tongue has a very rough surface. Cats' tongues are covered with small spikes called papillae. The papillae point backward and are used by the cat, together with its teeth, to scrape meat off bones. Around the edge and at the back of the tongue are taste buds. Cats cannot taste sweet things, and can actively recognize pure water.

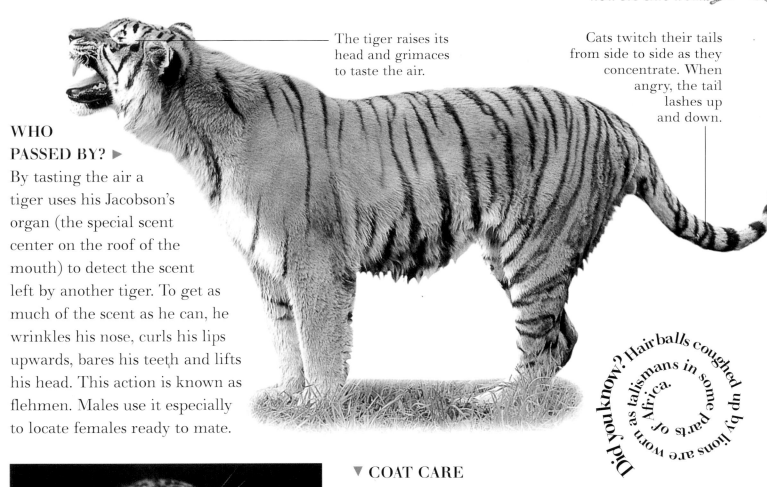

The tiger raises its head and grimaces to taste the air.

Cats twitch their tails from side to side as they concentrate. When angry, the tail lashes up and down.

WHO PASSED BY? ▶

By tasting the air a tiger uses his Jacobson's organ (the special scent center on the roof of the mouth) to detect the scent left by another tiger. To get as much of the scent as he can, he wrinkles his nose, curls his lips upwards, bares his teeth and lifts his head. This action is known as flehmen. Males use it especially to locate females ready to mate.

Did you know? Hairballs coughed up by lions are worn as talismans in some parts of Africa.

▲ CAT'S WHISKERS

This snow leopard's face is surrounded by sensitive whiskers. Cats use their whiskers to judge how far away objects are. The most important whiskers are on the sides of the face. These help a cat to feel its way in the dark, or when it is walking through tall grass.

▼ COAT CARE

The long, rough tongue of a lion makes a very good comb. It removes loose hairs and combs the fur flat and straight. Cats wipe their faces, coats and paws clean. They need to keep well groomed and spend a lot of time looking after their fur. Hair swallowed by grooming is spat out as hairballs.

Spots and Stripes

A cat's fur coat protects its skin and keeps it warm. The coat's colors and patterns help to camouflage (hide) the cat as it hunts prey. Wild cats' coats have two layers—an undercoat of short soft fur and an outercoat of tougher, longer hairs, called guard hairs. Together these two layers insulate the cat from extreme cold or extreme heat. Some guard hairs are sensitive and help a cat to feel its way. Cats have loose skin, making it difficult for an attacker to get a good grip and helping to prevent injury. The colors and patterns of a wild cat's coat depend on where it lives.

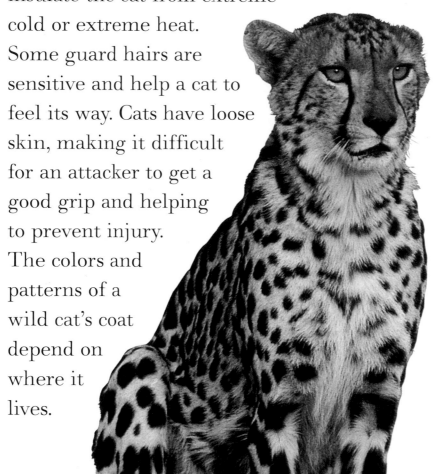

▲ TIGER IN THE GRASS

The stripes of a tiger's coat are the perfect camouflage for an animal that needs to prowl around in long grass. The colors and patterns help to make the cat almost invisible as it stalks its prey. These markings are also very effective in a leafy jungle where the dappled light makes stripes of light and shade.

Did you know? Domestic cats have a wider range of colors and markings than wild cats.

◄ KING OF THE HILL

King cheetahs were once thought to be different from other cheetahs. They have longer fur, darker colors and spots on their backs that join up to form stripes. Even so, they are the same species. All cheetahs have distinctive tear stripes running from the corners of their eyes down beside their muzzles.

▲ FRATERNAL TWINS

Many big cats of the same species come in variations of color, depending partly on where they live. These two leopard cubs are twins, but one has a much darker, blackish coat. Black leopards are called panthers. (Black jaguars and even pumas are sometimes called panthers.) Some leopards live deep in the shadows of the forest, where darker coloring helps them to hide more easily. Panthers are most common in Asia.

▼ SPOT THE DIFFERENCE

Spots, stripes or blotches break up the outline of a cat's body. This helps it to blend in with the shadows made by the leaves of bushes and trees, or the lines of tall grass. In the dappled light of a forest or in the long grass of the savanna, cats are very well hidden indeed.

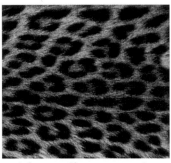

A leopard's spots are in fact small rosettes.

The tiger has distinctive black stripes.

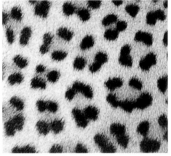

A jaguar has rosettes with a central spot of color.

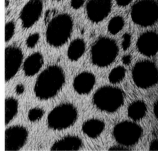

The cheetah has lots of spots and no rosettes.

◄ WHITE FOR SNOW

A snow leopard has a shaggy, off-white coat with darker spots. This coloring helps the snow leopard to stay well hidden in the rocky, mountainous terrain where it lives. It moves around early in the morning or late afternoon, blending with its habitat as it looks for prey.

A snow leopard's pale, thick coat has dark irregular spots and streaks. This helps it to hide between the rocks and snow.

21

On the Move

Cats run and jump easily and gracefully. They have flexible spines and long, strong hind legs. With long, bouncy strides, they can cover a lot of ground very quickly. Big cats are not good long-distance runners, they are sprinters and pouncers. They use their long tails for balance when climbing trees and running fast. All cats can swim very well, but some do not like the water and will only swim to escape danger. Others, such as tigers and jaguars, live near water and often swim to hunt their prey.

▲ THRILL OF THE CHASE
A lion chases its prey through the scrub. When lions stalk, run and pounce, they make use of their flexible backs, strong back legs, powerful chests and cushioning pads under their paws. Cats' back legs are especially powerful. They provide the major thrust for running. Cats can outpace their prey over short distances before launching into a final jump.

◄ TREE-CLIMBING CAT
Leopards spend a lot of time in trees and are designed for climbing. They have very powerful chests and front legs. Their shoulder blades are positioned to the side to make them better climbers. A leopard can leap almost 10 feet without difficulty and, in exceptional circumstances, can leap over 19½ feet.

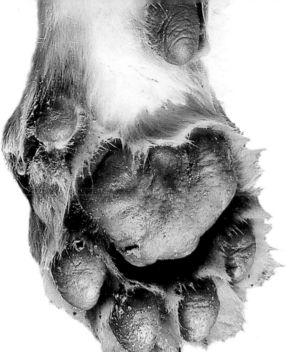

◄ SOFT PADDING

The thick pads under a lion's paw are like cushions. They allow the lion to move very quietly and also act as shock absorbers for running and jumping. Hidden between the pads and fur are the lion's claws, tucked away safely until they are needed.

GRACE AND AGILITY ►

A bobcat leaps with great agility off a rock. All cats have flexible backs and short collarbones to help make their bodies stronger for jumping off things. Bobcats are similar to lynxes. Both cats have an extensive coating of fur on their feet to give them extra warmth. The fur also prevents them from slipping on icy rocks.

Did you know? In the 1500s, rich people kept cheetahs as hunting animals like dogs.

As it leaps, a bobcat pinpoints its landing position. The front feet land separately in quick succession.

◄ KEEPING COOL CAT

A Bengal tiger swims gracefully across a river. Many tigers live in warm climates, such as India and Southeast Asia. As well as swimming to get from one place to another, they often look for pools of water to bathe in during the heat of the day. They are one of the few cats that actively enjoy being in or near water. Tigers are excellent swimmers and can easily cross a lake 3 miles wide.

Focus on the

A cheetah can run at 71 miles per hour over short distances—a speed equivalent to a fast car. This makes it the world's fastest land animal. The cheetah's body is fine-tuned for speed. It has wide nostrils to breathe in as much oxygen as possible and specially adapted paws for running fast. Most cheetahs today live in east and southern Africa, with a small number living in Asia—in Iran and Pakistan. They live in many different kinds of habitats, from open grassland to thick bush and even in desert-like environments.

1 A pair of cheetahs creeps up stealthily on a herd of antelope. Cheetahs hunt their prey by slinking toward the herd, holding their heads low. Cheetahs are not pouncing killers, like other cats. Instead, they pull down their prey after a very fast chase. In order to waste as little energy as possible, cheetahs plan their attack first. They pick out their target before starting the chase.

2 The cheetah begins its chase as the herd of antelope starts to move. It can accelerate from walking pace to around 43 miles per hour in two seconds. Cheetahs have retractable claws, but unlike other cats they have no protective sheaths. The uncovered claws act like the spikes on the bottom of track shoes, helping the cheetah to grip as it runs. Ridges on their paw pads also help to improve grip.

3 At top speed a cheetah makes full use of its flexible spine and lean, supple body. A cheetah's legs are very long and slender compared to its body. It can cover several yards in a single bound.

Hunting Cheetah

4 As the cheetah closes in on the herd, the antelope spring in all directions. The cheetah changes direction without slowing down. If a cheetah does not catch its prey within about a quarter of a mile, it has to give up the chase. Cheetahs usually hunt in the morning or late in the afternoon, when it is not too hot. They have short lifespans in the wild, because their speed declines with age, making it difficult to catch prey.

5 As the cheetah closes in on its prey it may have to make several sharp turns to keep up. The cheetah's long tail gives it excellent balance as it turns. The cheetah knocks its victim off balance with a swipe of its front paw. It uses its big dew claw to pull the victim to the ground.

6 Once the prey animal is down, the cheetah grabs the victim's throat. A sharp bite suffocates the antelope. Cheetahs are not strong enough to kill by biting through the spinal cord in the prey's neck like other cats. The cheetah will hang on to the victim's throat until the antelope is dead.

Communication

All big cats communicate with one another. They tell each other how old they are, whether they are male or female, what mood they are in and where they live. Cats communicate by signals such as smells, scratches and sounds. The smells come from urine and from scent glands. Cats have scent glands on their heads and chins, between their toes and at the base of their tails. Every time they rub against something, they transfer their special smell. Cats make many different sounds. Scientists know that cats speak to each other, but still do not understand much about their language. Cats also communicate using body language. They use their ears to signal their mood and twitch their tails to show if they are excited or agitated.

▲ A MIGHTY ROAR

The lion's roar is the loudest sound cats make. It is loud enough for all the "neighborhood" lions to hear. Lions roar after sunset, following a kill and when they have finished eating. Lions make at least nine different sounds. They also grunt to each other as they move around.

HISSING LEOPARD ▶

An angry leopard hisses at an enemy. Cats hiss and spit when they feel threatened, or when they are fighting an enemy. The position of a cat's ears also signals its intentions. When a cat is about to attack, it flattens its ears back against its neck.

EAR SIGNALS

Many wild cats, such as this tiger, have white markings on the back of their ears. They turn their ears to show the markings to an enemy when they are angry.

CAT SPRAY

A king cheetah marks its territory by spraying urine at points along its trails. Scent marks left by a male tell other males to stay away. The scent left by a female will tell a male passing through her range if she is ready to mate.

BABY TALK

Mothers talk to their cubs a lot. The sounds are quiet so that enemies do not hear. The softest and safest sound of all is purring.

MARKS FOR SHOW

Cats like to scratch things to clean their claws and stretch their limbs. At the same time they leave a scented mark for others to both see and smell. When this lioness scratches, she leaves her own personal scent from the glands between her toes on the scratch marks.

Did you know? When they are close together, lions chirrup, meow and yowl to each other.

Hunting Prey

All cats, big and small, are carnivores—they eat meat. Their bodies are not designed to digest plants. Big cats must hunt down and kill their own food. Most big cats, however, are only too happy to eat someone else's meal and steal kills from other animals whenever they can. Cheetahs are an exception, and eat only animals they have killed themselves. To catch and kill their food, big cats must hunt. Some, like cheetahs, patrol their territories, looking for prey. Others, such as jaguars, hide in wait and then ambush their victims. Many cats, such as leopards, do both.

King Solomon
Solomon ruled Israel in the 900s B.C. and was reputed to be a very wise ruler. His throne was carved with lions because of his admiration for these big cats who killed only out of necessity. In law, if a man was said to have fallen into a lions' den, it was not proof of his death.

◄ **THE MAIN COURSE**
A big lion can kill large, powerful animals like this buffalo. A big cat usually attacks from behind, or from the side. If the prey is too big to grab right away, the cat will knock it off balance, hold on to it and bite into its neck.

CHOOSING A MEAL ►
A herd of antelope and zebra grazes while keeping watch on a lioness crouched in the grass. She lies as close to the ground as possible, waiting to pounce. Finally, when focused on a victim, she will bring her hind legs back into position and dart forward.

28

▲ WARTHOG SPECIAL

Four cheetahs surround an injured warthog. The mother cheetah is teaching her three cubs hunting techniques. The cheetah on the right is trying a left paw sideswipe, while another tries using its dew claw. Cheetahs love to eat warthogs but also catch antelope and smaller animals such as hares.

▲ CAT AND MOUSE

A recently killed capybara (a large rodent) makes a tasty meal for a jaguar. Jaguars often catch their food in water, such as fish and turtles. On land they hunt armadillos, deer, opossums, skunks, snakes, squirrels, tortoises and monkeys.

Did you know? Cheetahs will only chase prey if it runs. If it stops, so does the cheetah.

SLOW FOOD ▶

If a lion has not been able to hunt successfully for a while, it will eat small creatures such as this tortoise. Lions usually hunt big animals such as antelope, wildebeest, warthogs, giraffe, buffalo, bush pigs and baboons. They work together in a group to hunt large prey.

Killing Prey

The way a big cat kills its prey depends on the size of the cat and the size of its meal. If the prey is small with a bite-sized neck, it will be killed with a bite through the spinal cord. If the prey has a bite-sized head, the cat will use its powerful jaws to crush the back of its skull. Large prey is killed by biting its throat and suffocating it. Lions often hunt together and use a combined effort to kill large prey. One lion may grab the prey's throat to suffocate it, while other lions attack from behind.

Did you know? Lions try to flip porcupines onto their backs to avoid the sharp spines.

▼ **OLD AGE**
When big cats get old or injured it is very difficult for them to hunt. They will eventually die from starvation. This lion from the Kalahari Desert in South Africa is old and thin. It has been weakened by hunger.

◀ **FAIR GAME**
A warthog is a small, delicious meal for a cheetah. The bigger the cat, the bigger its prey. A cheetah is quite a light cat, so to kill an animal the cheetah first knocks it over, then bites the prey's neck to suffocate it.

▲ **A DEADLY EMBRACE**
A lioness immobilizes a struggling wildebeest by biting its windpipe and suffocating it to death. Lions are very strong animals. A lion weighing 330 to 550 pounds can kill a buffalo more than twice its weight. Female lions do most of the hunting for their pride.

◄ SECRET STASH

A cheetah carrying off its prey, a young gazelle, to a safe place. Once it has killed, a cheetah will check the area to make sure it is secure before feeding. It drags the carcass to a covered spot in the bushes. Here it can eat its meal hidden from enemies. Cheetahs are often driven off and robbed of their kills by hyenas and jackals or even other big cats.

A SOLID MEAL ►

These cheetahs will devour as much of this antelope as they can. Big cats lie on the ground and hold their food with their forepaws when they eat. When they have satisfied their hunger, cheetahs cover up or hide the carcass with grass, leaves or whatever is available in order to save it for later.

LIONS' FEAST ►

A pride of lions gather around their kill, a zebra. They eat quickly before any scavenging hyenas and vultures can steal the meat. Each lion has its place in the pride. Even if they are very hungry, they must wait until it is their turn to eat. Usually the dominant male lion eats first.

Focus on the Lone

Leopards are one of the most widespread of all the big cats, but are also the most mysterious. They live in many different habitats throughout Africa and southern Asia, in open, rocky country as well as in forests. Not much is known about them because they are nocturnal animals, coming out to hunt at night. They sometimes creep up on prey on the ground, then pounce. At other times they ambush their prey from a tree.

CAT NAP
Leopards usually sleep all day in a tree, especially when it is very hot. Their spotted coat is excellent camouflage in the patchwork of light and shade in the forest. It is so good that, when they are resting, they are especially hard to see.

LONE LEOPARD
Leopards are loners. They come together only when a female signals to a male that she is ready to mate. After mating they separate again. The mother brings up the cubs until they are able to fend for themselves.

Leopard

BRUTE STRENGTH

A leopard drags its dead victim across the ground. Leopards have strong jaws, chests and front legs so that they can move an animal as big as themselves.

AMBUSH

Leopards like to ambush prey. They climb onto a low branch and wait for an animal to walk underneath. Then they jump down and grab it. The leopard uses its great strength to drag its victim high up into the tree. Prey includes pigs, antelope, monkeys, dogs and many other animals.

TOP MEAL

This leopard has dragged its kill up into a tree. This is to prevent the carcass from being stolen. Other big carnivores that live in the same area cannot climb trees as well as leopards. Once the prey is safe, a leopard can finish its meal.

Living Together

Most big cats live alone. They hunt alone and the females bring up their cubs alone. Big cats come together only when they want to mate. They are solitary because of the prey that they hunt. There is usually not enough prey in one area for a large group of big cats to live on. Lions are the exception. They live in family groups called prides. (Male cheetahs also sometimes live in groups with up to four members.) All wild cats have territories (home ranges). These territories are a series of trails that link together a cat's hunting area, its drinking places, its lookout positions and the den where it brings up its young. Females have smaller home ranges than males. Males that have more than one mate have territories that overlap with two or more female home ranges.

Did you know? Big cats' territories range from a few square miles to over 1,000.

▲ **BRINGING UP BABY**

Female snow leopards bring up their cubs on their own. They have up to five cubs who stay with their mother for at least a year. Although snow leopards are loners, they are not unsociable. They like to live near each other and let other snow leopards cross their territories.

◄ **THE LOOKOUT**

A puma keeps watch over its territory from a hill. Pumas are solitary and deliberately avoid each other except during courtship and mating. The first male puma to arrive in an area claims it as his territory. He chases out any other male that tries to live there.

▲ A PRIDE OF LIONS

The lions in a pride drink together, hunt together, eat together and play together. A pride is usually made up of related females and their young. Prides usually try not to meet up with other prides. To tell the others to keep out of its territory, the pride leaves scent markings on the edge of its range.

Daniel and the Lions' Den
A story in the Bible tells how Daniel was taken prisoner by Nebuchadnezzar, king of Babylon. When Daniel correctly interpreted the king's dreams he became a favorite of the king. His enemies became jealous of his position and had him thrown into a lions' den, a common punishment for prisoners at the time. But instead of eating Daniel, the lions befriended him. They were tamed by his great faith in God.

▲ FAMILY GROUPS

A cheetah mother sits between her two cubs. The cubs will stay with her until they are about 18 months old. The female then lives a solitary life. Males, however, live in small groups and defend a territory. They only leave their range if there is a drought or if food is very scarce.

▲ WELL GROOMED

Cats that live together groom each other. They do this to be friendly and to keep clean. They also groom to spread their scent on each other, so that they smell the same. This helps them to recognize each other and identify strangers.

Focus on

Lions are the second largest of the big cats after tigers. They like to live in open spaces, sometimes in woodlands, but never in tropical forests. Lions are usually found on the savannas (grassy plains) and on the edges of deserts. Female lions live together in prides (family groups) of up to 12 lionesses and their cubs. The size of the group depends on how much food there is available. Male lions may live together in groups, called coalitions, which look after one or more prides. The coalitions defend their prides, fighting off any other males who want to mate with the females of their pride.

FATHER AND SON

Male lions are the only big cats that look different from the females. They have long shaggy manes to look larger and fiercer and to protect their necks in a fight.
A male cub starts to grow a mane at about the age of three. At that age he also leaves the pride to establish his own territory.

THE FAMILY

A pride of lions rests near a waterhole. The biggest prides live in open grasslands where there are large herds of antelope, wildebeest and buffalo. If a foreign male takes over a pride, the new lion kills all the cubs under six months old. This is to ensure all the cubs are his.

a Pride

NURSERY SCHOOL

Young lions play tag to learn how to chase things and defend their pride. The pride does not usually allow strange lions to join the family group. Young lions need to be prepared in case other lions come to fight with them.

FIRST AT THE TABLE

Male lions usually eat first, even though the females do most of the hunting. He can eat up to 65 pounds of meat at one time, but will not need to eat again for several days.

CAT SCRAP

Two lionesses fight each other to decide who will be first to eat. There is usually a dominant female in each pride, even when there are males around. This chief female rules the family.

MOTHER AND CUBS

Lionesses give birth to a litter of between one and six cubs. The cubs start learning to hunt when they are about 11 months old, but stay with their mother for over two years. In dry areas, lions live in small prides because less food is available.

Lionesses help to raise the young together. They even suckle each other's cubs.

Finding a Mate

Big cats roam over large areas, so it can be quite difficult for them to find a partner. When they are ready to mate, they use scent markers. These are like advertisements to all the other cats in the district. A female also calls loudly, in the hope that a nearby male will come to her. Often more than one male will follow a female. This almost always leads to fights between the interested males. The winner of the fight then begins to court the female. In a pride of lions, one male establishes his dominance over the group. In this way he avoids having to fight every time a female is ready to mate. Many big cats will mate several times a day for up to a week to make sure that the female is pregnant.

▲ COURTSHIP

A male lion rubs against a female and smells her all over. He knows that the lioness is ready to mate from her scent. Having fought off rivals, he must now persuade the lioness to mate with him. He courts her by being attentive. Their courtship may last for several days before they mate.

Did you know? Pumas are also called mountain screamers after the female's mating call.

◄ THE MATING COUPLE

When the female is ready to mate, she crouches on the ground with her hindquarters slightly raised. The male sits behind and over her and sometimes holds the scruff of her neck between his jaws. Large cats, such as leopards and lions, may mate up to 100 times a day. Smaller cats, such as cheetahs, are more vulnerable to predators and so mate for a shorter time.

KEEPING HIM IN HIS PLACE ▶

After mating, the lioness is aggressive and often lashes out at the lion. As soon as the two have mated the male jumps back very quickly. He remains close by her side to stop other males from approaching. Once she has calmed down she rolls on her back and they mate again. Each mating lasts only a few seconds.

Did you know? A wild big cat may have up to 5 litters in an average lifespan of 12 years.

▲ LEAN AND HEALTHY

This lioness is only just pregnant. She has not put on much weight and can still hunt efficiently. At the end of her pregnancy (about three to four months) she will hunt small, easy-to-catch prey. Lionesses in a pride also get to share in the pride's kill.

▼ CAT ATTRACTION

Two courting tigers often make a great deal of noise. They roar, meow, moan and grunt as they mate. Female tigers mate every other year. The male stays close by the female for a few days until he is sure she is pregnant. Then the pair separate and live on their own again.

Giving Birth

The cubs (babies) of a big cat are usually born with spotted fur and closed eyes. They are completely helpless. The mother cat looks after them on her own with no help from the father. She gives birth in a safe place called a den. For the first few days after birth, she stays very close to her cubs so that they can feed on her milk. She keeps them warm and cleans the cubs by licking them all over. The cubs grow quickly. Even before their eyes open they can crawl, and they soon learn to hiss to defend themselves.

▲ SNOW CUB

Snow leopard cubs have white fur with dark spots. They are always born in the spring and open their eyes one week after birth. The cubs begin to follow their mothers around when they are about three months old. By winter, they will be almost grown up.

MOTHERLY LOVE ▶

Tiger cubs are capable killers by the time they are 11 months old. They stay with their mothers, however, until they are two or even three years of age. In the wild, the mother does all she can to protect her young, but often at least half of the litter dies. Predators may kill the cubs, or sometimes they starve to death if the mother cannot catch enough food.

IN DISGUISE ▶
A cheetah cub is covered in long, woolly fur. This makes it look similar to the African honey badger, a very fierce animal, which may help to discourage predators. The mother cheetah does not raise her cubs in a den, but moves them around every few days.

A cheetah cub, unlike the adult, has a mane of fur. This may help to disguise it as it hides in the long grass.

▲ BRINGING UP BABY
Female pumas give birth to up to six kittens (babies). The mother has several pairs of teats for the kittens to suckle from. Each kitten has its own teat and will use no other. They will suckle her milk for at least three months and from about six weeks they will also eat meat.

▲ ON GUARD
Two lionesses guard the entrance to their den. Lions are social cats and share the responsibility of keeping guard. Dens are kept very clean so that there are no smells to attract predators.

▲ MOVING TO SAFETY
If at any time a mother cat thinks her cubs are in danger, she will move them to a new den. She carries the cubs one by one, gently grasping the loose skin at their necks between her teeth.

41

Focus on

The number of cubs in a big cat's litter depends on the species and where it lives. Most big cats have two or three cubs, but cheetahs have five or more. All cubs are born helpless, but it is not long before their eyes open and they can wobble around, learning to balance on their uncertain legs. Within a few weeks they begin to play with their mothers and each other. There is a lot to find out, but they learn very quickly. By the time they are six months old they will have learned how to keep themselves safe, what food tastes good and how to catch it. They will start to understand the language of smells and sounds. For the next year and a half they will stay close to their mothers, practicing their new skills until they are experts.

PLAY TIME
A cub plays with its mother's tail. As soon as cubs can see, they begin to play. Play helps to build up muscles, improve coordination and develop good reflexes. It is valuable early preparation for learning how to hunt when the cubs are older.

SAFETY FIRST
For the first two years of their lives, cubs remain close to their mothers. She protects them and helps them when they make mistakes. A mother may rear all of her cubs successfully in a good year. She may lose most or even all of her cubs, depending on her skills as a parent and the availability of food.

BATH TIME
Cubs must learn to clean themselves, but while they are still young their mother washes them with her tongue. As she licks, she spreads her scent on the cubs so that all of her family have the same smell.

Cute Cubs

FAMILY BLISS

Lion cubs are spotted all over to help hide them from predators. The spots gradually fade as the lions grow older. Adult lions have only very faint spots on their legs and stomachs. Lion cubs are lucky because they have many companions to play with. Cubs of solitary cats have to grow up without much company. Some do not even have any brothers or sisters. Lion cubs learn through play how to get along with other lions.

MOVING HOME

To move her cubs a lioness carries each one gently in her mouth. Not only do the cubs have loose skin at their necks, but the lioness has a special gap in her mouth behind the canines. This allows her to lift the cub off the ground without biting it.

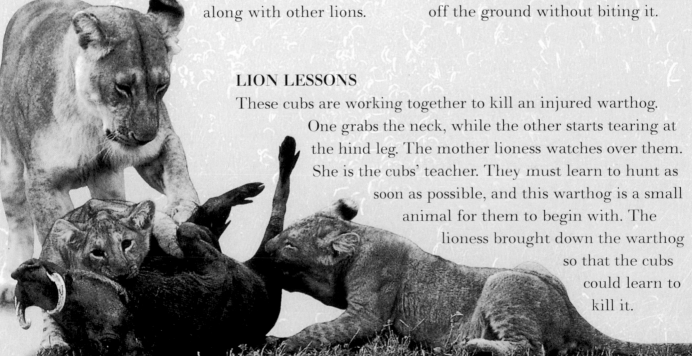

LION LESSONS

These cubs are working together to kill an injured warthog. One grabs the neck, while the other starts tearing at the hind leg. The mother lioness watches over them. She is the cubs' teacher. They must learn to hunt as soon as possible, and this warthog is a small animal for them to begin with. The lioness brought down the warthog so that the cubs could learn to kill it.

Growing Up

Young cubs have to learn all about life as an adult so that they can look after themselves when they leave their mother. She teaches them as much as she can, and the rest they learn through play. Cub games depend on their species, because each type of cat has different things to learn. In play-fighting cheetahs use their paws to knock each other over. This is a technique they will need for hunting when they are older. Cubs need to learn how to judge distances and when to strike to kill prey quickly, without getting injured or killed themselves. Their mother introduces them to prey by bringing an animal back to the den to eat. Mothers and cubs use very high-pitched sounds to communicate. However, if she senses danger, she growls at them to tell them to hide.

▲ **PRACTICE MAKES PERFECT**
These cheetah cubs are learning to kill a Thomson's gazelle. When the cubs are about 12 weeks old, a mother cheetah brings back live injured prey for them to kill. They instinctively know how to do so, but need practice to get it right.

▼ **FOLLOW MY LEADER**
Curious cheetah cubs watch an object intently, safe beside their mother. At about six weeks the cubs start to go on hunting trips with her. They are able to keep up by following her white-tipped tail through the tall grass.

THE CLASSROOM ▶

A group of lion cubs relax in the shade on a fallen tree. From here they watch the adults hunt, as if in a big, open-air classroom. Female cubs often stay in the pride, but young males are chased off by the dominant male.

◀ SCRATCH AND SNIFF

Three young lions sniff at the shell of a tortoise. Cubs learn to be cautious when dealing with unfamiliar objects. First the object is tapped with a paw, before being explored further with the nose. Cubs' milk teeth are replaced with permanent canine teeth at about two years old. Not until then can they begin to hunt and kill big animals.

TAIL TOY ▶

A mother leopard's tail is a good thing for her cub to learn to pounce on. She twitches it so the cub can develop good coordination and timing. As the cub grows, it will practice on rodents and then bigger animals until it can hunt for itself. Once they leave their mothers, female cubs usually establish a territory close by, while males go farther away.

45

Enemies of Big Cats

Big cats are perfect killing machines and are feared by all their prey. They do, however, have enemies. Big cats have to watch out for other carnivores taking their food or attacking their cubs. Wolves are a problem for pumas, wild dogs are a threat to tigers, and hyenas and jackals prey on the cubs of African big cats. Even prey animals can be a danger to big cats. Buffaloes are very aggressive and can attack and kill a young lion. Humans, however, are the main enemies of wild cats. As people move farther into the wilderness to build homes and farms, they destroy the precious habitats of the big cats. People kill the big cats' prey, leaving them with less to eat. They also hunt big cats for their beautiful and valuable fur coats.

▲ **SCAVENGING HYENAS**
A spotted hyena finishes off the remains of a giraffe. Hyenas live in Africa and western Asia. They eat whatever they can find. This is often carrion (the remains of dead prey) that animals such as big cats have killed for themselves. They will also kill cubs. Hyenas have strong jaws and bone-crunching teeth and look for food at night.

Did you know? Despite their dog-like appearance, hyenas are more closely related to cats.

◄ **PACK POWER**
Wolves live in Europe and North America. They live in the mountains as well as on open plains and hunt in packs of up to 20 animals. Wolves usually eat deer, elk, moose, or small animals such as hares. But they never ignore a good meal caught by a puma.

BIG CAT THREAT ▶

Leopards live in the same areas as cheetahs, but they are very hostile toward them. In fact, if they get a chance, leopards prey on cheetahs and their cubs. In turn, leopards have to be very wary of lions. Lions will attack and kill a leopard to protect the pride or their territory. Big cats do not like others because of competition for food in an area.

▲ **HUMAN TRAPS**

Experts examine a tiger trap. Poachers (people who kill animals illegally) often use traps to catch big cats. When the trap snaps shut, the animal is stuck until it dies or until the poacher returns to kill it. These traps cause great pain. A cat may try to chew off its trapped leg to escape.

▼ **DOG-LIKE JACKALS**

Jackals (a relative of the dog) are half the size of hyenas and live in Africa. They will eat most things and will steal a big cat's kill. If they come across an unprotected den, they quickly kill and eat all the cubs.

◀ **INTRUDER PERIL**

Sometimes big cats become cannibals and eat their own kind. These cheetahs are eating another cheetah that has invaded their territory. Male lions also eat all the young cubs in a pride when they take over dominance from another male.

Mountain Cats

To live in the mountains, cats need to be hardy and excellent rock climbers. They also have to cope with high altitudes where the air is thin and there is less oxygen to breathe. Big cats that live in the mountains include leopards and the rare snow leopard. Small cats include the puma, mountain cat, bobcat and lynx. Mountain climates are harsh, and the weather can change very quickly. To survive, mountain cats need to use their wits and to know where to find shelter. They mate so that their cubs are born in the spring. This is to ensure that they will be almost grown by the time winter arrives.

This map shows the world's major mountain ranges. The puma, mountain cat and lynx live in the Americas. Lynx also live in Europe and Asia, while the snow leopard lives in Asia.

▲ **MOUNTAIN CAT**
The mountain cat is a secretive, shy creature and seldom seen. It is about 1½ feet long and has soft, fine fur. It is also known as the Andean mountain cat, since it lives in the high Andes mountains of Chile, Argentina, Peru and Bolivia. This cat is found at altitudes of 16,000 feet above sea level.

◄ **MOUNTAIN LION**
A puma keeps watch over its vast territory. Pumas are also known as mountain lions and cougars. Male pumas can grow to 6½ feet long, and weigh 220 pounds. They are good at jumping and can easily leap 16 feet onto a high rock or into a tree. Pumas are found over a wide area, from Canada to the very tip of South America. They live along the foothills of mountains, in forests on mountain slopes and all the way up to 15,000 feet above sea level. Depending on where they live, pumas will eat deer, porcupines, hares, beavers and armadillos.

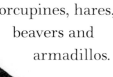

WINTER LYNX ▶

Lynx live in
mountainous
regions of Europe,
Asia and North
America. They have
unusually short tails
and tufted ears. Lynx are
well designed to live in very
cold places. In winter they
grow an especially long coat,
which is light colored so that
they are well camouflaged in
the snow. The bobcat of
North America looks
similar to the lynx.

PUMA CHASE

A snowshoe hare darts this
way and that to shake off a
puma. To catch the hare, the
puma must make full use of
its flexible back and its long
balancing tail. Pumas hunt
by day as well as by night.

LONG-TAILED SNOW LEOPARD ▶

The snow leopard is one of the rarest big cats,
found only in the Himalaya and Altai mountains
of central Asia. It can live at 20,000 feet, the
highest of any wild cat. Snow leopards feed
on wild goats, hares and marmots. Their bodies
measure just over 3¼ feet long, with tails that
are almost as long. They wrap their bushy tails
around themselves to keep warm when they
are sleeping. Snow leopards are agile jumpers and
said to be able to leap over gaps of 50 feet. Their
tails help them to balance as
they jump.

Did you know? A female snow leopard makes her den cosy by lining it with her own fur.

Forest Dwellers

Dense, wet rainforests are home to lots of small creatures, such as insects and spiders. These animals and forest plants provide a feast for birds, snakes, frogs and small mammals, which in turn are a banquet for big cats. Jaguars, tigers, leopards and clouded leopards all live in rainforests. Small cats include ocelots and margays. Although there is plenty of food in a forest, the dense trees make it a difficult place to hunt. There is little space among the trees and prey can escape easily in the thick undergrowth.

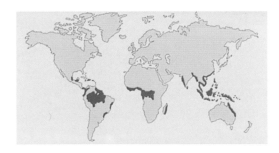

This map shows where the world's tropical rainforests are located. They lie in a band on either side of the Equator.

▼ OUT OF REACH

Leopards live in Africa and southern Asia in all kinds of habitat, from rainforest to dry grassland. They are great climbers and often drag their prey high into trees where they can be safe from thieving hyenas.

▲ CLOUDED LEOPARD

The clouded leopard is a shy and rarely seen Asian big cat. It lives in forests from Nepal to Borneo, spending most of its time in the trees. The Chinese call the clouded leopard the mint leopard because of its unusual leaf-like markings. Male clouded leopards reach about 3¼ feet long, with an equally long tail, and weigh about 65 pounds. They are perfectly built for tree climbing, with a long, bushy tail for balance and flexible ankle joints.

Did you know? The jaguar was the symbol of the Sun for the Maya of Central America.

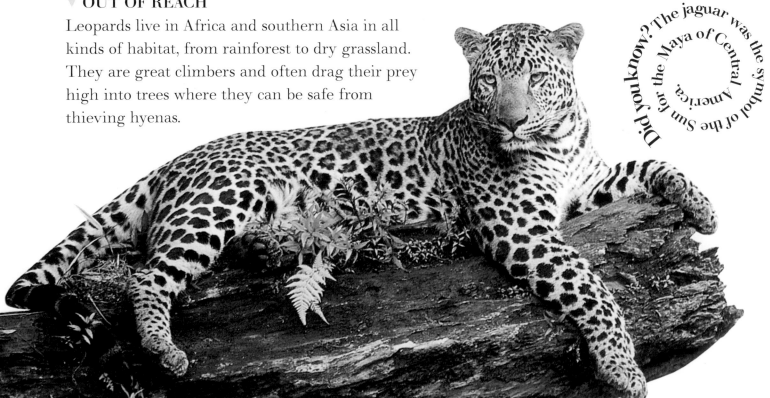

SUMATRAN TIGER

A tiger walks stealthily into a jungle pool on the island of Sumatra. Tigers are good swimmers, and a forest pool is a good place to hunt as well as to cool off from the tropical heat. Tigers often hide the carcasses of their prey in water or the dense undergrowth.

The sleek margay is very striking in appearance, with beautifully marked fur and large eyes.

MARGAY

Margays live in the tropical forests of Central and South America. They are the best of all cat climbers, with broad, soft feet and exceptionally flexible ankles and hind legs. They feed largely on birds and so need to be good at moving around in the tops of trees.

LOSS OF HABITAT

Jaguars can be found all over South and Central America but they prefer thick forests. They are threatened by over-hunting and the destruction of their forest habitat.

A TURTLE TREAT

A jaguar catches a river turtle in a pool. Jaguars are such good swimmers that they hunt some of their prey in water. They love to eat fish and turtles. Their jaws are powerful enough to crack open a turtle's shell like a nut. They have been known to kill cayman (a type of crocodile).

BLACK JAGUAR

Forest jaguars are darker than their grassland cousins. Some can be black and are so well camouflaged that they can disappear in the shadows of their forest habitat.

Focus on

Tigers are the largest of all the big cats, and the largest of all tigers is the Siberian tiger. An adult male can reach up to $8\frac{1}{2}$ feet long and weigh as much as 600 pounds. Siberian tigers live in the snow-covered forests of Siberia, which is part of Russia, and Manchuria in China. They are also sometimes known as Amur tigers. Although there is only one species of tiger, they can differ significantly in their appearance. Siberian tigers have a relatively pale coat with few stripes. Bengal tigers from India, however, have shorter fur and are more strikingly marked. As humans destroy more of their habitats, the number of tigers in the wild is declining dramatically. Today, there are only about 400 Siberian tigers left in the wild.

SOLITARY SIBERIAN
Siberian tigers live alone in huge territories of over 350 square miles. They do not like to fight and try to avoid each other. A tiger will kill another if it invades its territory.

OPEN WIDE
A Siberian tiger shows its long, sharp canine teeth in a wide yawn. Canines are used to catch and kill prey. Tigers kill ambushed prey by biting the neck or strangling it.

LUNCH TIME
A group of Siberian tigers devours a black ox. Despite being solitary animals, tigers do sometimes share food. The only other time they come together is to mate. Tigers have been known to roar when they have killed a big animal, just as lions will often roar when they have successfully caught their prey.

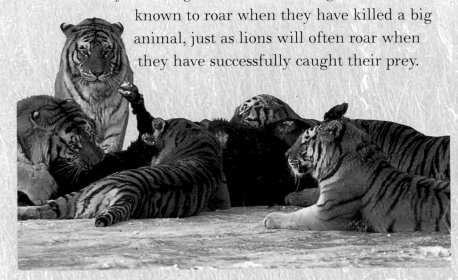

Siberian Tigers

ICY DRINK
A mother shows her 18-month-old cub how to drink water from melted ice. Tigers have up to four cubs in a litter, every other year. They stay with her for at least two years.

COURTING COUPLE
When a female is ready to mate, she sprays, roars and grunts to tell the male. When tigers want to be friendly, they blow sharply through their nostrils and mouths, rub their heads together and gently bite each other's necks.

A PALE ICE QUEEN
Siberian tigers like this female have a lot of white fur. This makes it more difficult for prey and enemies to see them in the snow. They are powerfully and heavily built, with bodies slung close to the ground.

On the Savanna

Savannas are open, flat areas of grassland. Apart from grasses, the main plants of the savanna are small bushes and clumps of trees. Savanna is the ideal habitat for big herds of grazing animals, such as antelope, zebra and buffalo. In Africa, these herds migrate for thousands of miles each year in search of fresh grass and water. They are followed by lions, cheetahs and leopards who prey on the herds. The savanna of South America is home to jaguars. Rodents, such as mice, gerbils and marmots, also thrive on the savanna and these are a good food source for smaller cats, such as the serval.

▲ LION IN THE GRASS

A lion walks through the long, dry grass of the African savanna. Its sandy coloring perfectly matches its habitat. Lions hunt their prey using the cover of grass. Often, only the tips of a lion's ears are seen as it slowly stalks its prey.

This map shows where the world's savannas (tropical grasslands and dry woodlands) are located. The largest region of savanna lies in Africa.

Did you know? Cats sleep for longer than most other animals. Lions sleep for 20 hours a day.

◄ CHEETAH ON THE LOOKOUT

A cheetah stands on the top of a small mound on the Kenyan savanna. Cheetahs are perfectly adapted for life on the plains. The surrounding open, flat terrain lets them make the most of their ability to chase down prey. From its vantage point, a cheetah uses its excellent eyesight to search for prey. It also keeps watch for any other cheetahs who might have invaded its home range.

◀ VIEW FROM A BRANCH

Leopards like to live in areas of grassland where there are trees. Here they can sleep hidden during the heat of the day. They can also enjoy the afternoon breeze and avoid the insects that live in the grass below. Leopards also prefer to eat up in a tree, out of the reach of scavengers.

Leo the Lion

People born between July 24 and August 23 are born under the astrological sign of Leo (the lion). They are said to be brave, strong and proud, just like lions.

▲ AT THE WATERHOLE

During the dry season in the African savanna, many grazing animals gather near waterholes to drink. Thomson's gazelle, zebra and giraffe are shown here. Lions congregate around the waterholes, not only to drink, but also to catch prey unaware. Their favorite prey is antelope, buffalo, zebra and warthog, but they also eat giraffe.

SPEEDY SERVAL ▶

Servals are small cats that live on the savanna of western and central Africa. They like to live near water where there are bushes to hide in. The servals' long legs enable them to leap over tall grass when they hunt small rodents. They also climb well and hunt birds. With their long legs, servals can run quickly over short distances and so escape from predators.

Desert Cats

Hot deserts are very dry places. Although they are hot during the day, at night they are very cold. Few plants and animals can survive in such a harsh environment, but cats are very adaptable. Cheetahs, lions and leopards live in the Kalahari and Namib deserts of southern Africa. As long as there are animals to eat, the cats can survive. Even the jaguar, a cat that loves water, has been seen in desert areas in Mexico and the southern United States. But they are only visitors in this tough, dry land and soon go back to the wetter places they prefer. The most well-adapted cat to desert life is a small cat known as the sand cat. It lives in the northern Sahara Desert, the Middle East and western Asia.

Did you know? Lions follow along dry riverbeds looking for waterholes in the desert.

This map shows where the world's hot deserts and nearby semi-desert areas are located.

▲ **DESERT STORM**

Two lions endure a sandstorm in the Kalahari Desert of southern Africa. The desert is a very hostile place to live. There is very little water, not much food and the wind blows up terrible sandstorms. Despite these hardships, big cats like these lions manage to survive.

▼ **A HARSH LIFE**

An old lion drinks from a waterhole in the Kalahari Desert. Even when a big cat lives in a dry place, it still needs to find enough water to drink. This is often a difficult task, requiring the animals to walk long distances. In the desert, prey is usually very spread out, so an old lion has a hard time trying to feed itself adequately.

▲ CHEETAH WALK

A group of cheetahs walk across the wide expanse of the Kalahari Desert. They lead lives of feast and famine. In the rainy season, lush vegetation grows, and enormous herds of antelope can graze. The cheetahs have a banquet preying on the grazing herds. But they go very hungry as the land dries up and prey becomes scarce.

◀ **SAND CAT**

Dense hair on the pads of the sand cat's feet protects it as it walks on hot ground and helps it to walk on loose sand. All the water the cat needs comes from its food, so it does not need to drink.

Big ears hear the soft, high-pitched squeaks of rodents.

Very thick, soft fur protects from the heat and cold.

▲ ADAPTABLE LEOPARD

A leopard rolls in the desert sand. There are very few trees in the desert, so leopards live among rocky outcrops. Here they can drag their prey to high places to eat in safety. The desert can be a dangerous place. With so little food around, competition can be fierce, especially with hungry lions. Big cats will eat small prey such as insects to keep from starving.

Egyptian Cat Worship
The Ancient Egyptians kept cats to protect their stores of grain from rats and mice. Cats became so celebrated that they were worshipped as gods. They were sacred to the cat-headed goddess of pleasure, Bast. Many cats were given funerals when they died. Their bodies were preserved, wrapped in bandages and richly painted.

Killer Cats

Humans can sometimes become the prey of big cats. People have been afraid of big cats for thousands of years. From 20,000-year-old cave paintings we know that people lived in contact with big cats and almost certainly feared them. More recently, there have been many reports of big cats killing people. Lions and tigers become bold when they are hungry and there is little other food around. First, they prey on livestock, such as cattle. When the cattle are gone, the big cats might kill people. Leopards, who do not have a natural fear of humans, may have their killer instinct triggered by an injury.

▲ LION BAITING

The Romans used lions (and bears) for gladiator fights in their amphitheaters (outdoor arenas). When the Romans wanted to kill prisoners, they would feed them to hungry lions. The lions had to be starving and made angry by their handlers, otherwise they would not kill the prisoners. Most captive lions will not kill people.

◄ WRESTLING A TIGER

Tigers are considered the most dangerous of all the big cats. This picture, called *A Timely Rescue*, shows a rather heroic view of killing a tiger. Once a tiger has become used to the taste of human flesh, it will strike at any time. Tigers have killed thousands of people over the centuries. During the early 1900s, tigers killed 800 to 900 people a year in India.

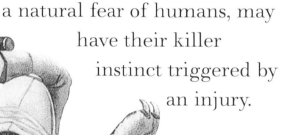

Did you know? In the early 1900s, one Indian leopard killed 125 people in eight years.

▲ TIPPU'S TIGER

This mechanical toy of a tiger attacking a British soldier was made in 1790. It is called Tippu's Tiger and was made for the Sultan of Mysore.

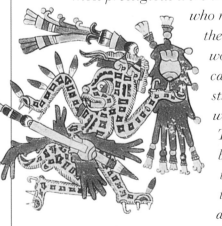

◄ HUNTER WITH A HEART

Jim Corbett was a famous hunter who lived in India in the early 1900s. Unlike most hunters of his day, he did not kill big cats for sport. He shot tigers and leopards that had been eating people.

Jaguar Knights

In the 1500s in Central America, Aztec warriors were divided into military orders. Some of the most prestigious were the jaguar knights who ranked just below the emperor. They wore entire wild cats' pelts, with the still-attached heads worn as helmets. They thought that by wearing the pelt they would take on the cat's strength and stealth.

▲ EDUCATION FOR CONSERVATION

Nearly 100 tigers and 50 leopards live in the Corbett National Park in India. The Park runs programs to teach children all about the big cats and their habitat. The more we know about big cats, the better able we are to respect them.

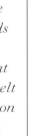

Cats in Danger

The earliest record that we have of people using wild-cat pelts (skins) is from 6500BC. It comes from the archaeological site of Çatal Hüyük in Turkey where there is evidence that dancers wore leopard skins. Much more recently, in the 1800s and 1900s, many wealthy people wanted to hunt big game for the thrill of the chase. Big cat skins were used to decorate the hunters' houses, and their heads hung as trophies on the walls. Today, no one is allowed to hunt the endangered big cats any more.

▲ LION HUNT

Egyptian rulers hunted lions from horse-drawn chariots. Hieroglyphics (picture writing) tell us of Pharaoh Amenophis III (1405–1367BC) who killed over 100 lions in the ten years of his rule. Some experts now think that the Egyptians may have bred lions specially to hunt them.

TIGER-HUNTING PRINCE ▶

This old painting on cotton shows an Indian prince hunting a tiger from the back of his elephant. Tiger hunting was a very popular pastime for many centuries in India until it was declared illegal in the 1970s.

▲ RITUAL ROBES

The Zulu chief Mangosothu Buthelezi
wears wild cat skins on special occasions,
like many African leaders and tribal healers.
They are a sign of his rank and high status.

▼ GREAT WHITE HUNTER

A hunting party proudly displays its tiger trophy.
This photograph was taken in the 1860s. When
India was under British rule, tiger hunting was
considered to be a great sport by the British.
Uncontrolled, ruthless hunting was a major cause
of the tiger's dramatic fall in numbers.

Did you know? Until the 1800s, black panthers lived near Los Angeles, California.

◄ CAT'S SKIN

A leopard is skinned,
having been shot in the Okavango
Delta in Botswana. Some game
reserves raise money for
conservation by charging huge
sums to hunt. This only happens
when numbers of a certain species
are too large for the reserve.

SECOND SKIN ►

Some people continue to think it
looks good to wear a coat made from
the pelts of a wild cat. Many more,
however, think that the fur looks
much better on the cat. Designers
now use fake fur and skins dyed
to look like pelts, instead.

Protecting Cats

All big cats are in danger of extinction. They are hunted not only for their skins, but also for their teeth, bones and other body parts, which are used as traditional medicines in many countries. The Convention for International Trade in Endangered Species (CITES) lists all big cats under Appendix 1, which strictly controls their import and export. For cats particularly at risk, such as the tiger, all trade is banned. There are now many protected areas throughout the world where big cats can live without human interference. These areas are often not big enough, however, so the cats leave in search of food. They attack livestock and sometimes the local farmers.

▲ **IN ANCIENT TIMES**
A Roman mosaic showing a horseman hunting a leopard. Two thousand years ago, big cats were much more widespread. Until the 1900s, cheetahs lived throughout Africa, central India and the Middle East. Hunting big cats was not a problem when there were many big cats and not so many people, but now the situation is desperate.

▲ **GIR NATIONAL PARK**
The last remaining Asian lions live in the Gir National Park in western India. There are fewer than 300 lions living in the park. The Asian lion is slightly different to the African lion. It has a smaller mane and a fold of skin running between its front and back legs.

▲ **SERENGETI LION PROJECT**
This lion has been drugged so that it can be fitted with a radio collar, checked and then released. In the Serengeti National Park in Tanzania, scientists use methods like this to study lion behavior.

▲ TIGER DETERRENT

Villagers in the Sundarbans mangrove forests in India wear masks on the backs of their heads. Tigers attack from behind, but will not usually strike if they see a face. The largest remaining tiger population in India is in the Sundarbans. Here 50 to 60 people die each year from attacks by tigers. There is obviously not enough food for the tigers, so conservationists are trying to improve the situation. Another deterrent is to set up dummies that look and smell like humans, but give out an electric shock if attacked. There are also electrified fences in some areas, and pigs are bred and released as tiger food.

▼ RADIO TRACKING

Biologists attach a radio collar to a tigress in the Chitwan National Park in Nepal. To save wild cats we need to understand their habits and their needs. For this reason, many scientists and conservationists are studying them. It is a very difficult task since cats are secretive and often nocturnal animals. One way of gathering information is to put a radio collar on a big cat and then follow its movements. By doing this, the animal can be tracked at long range.

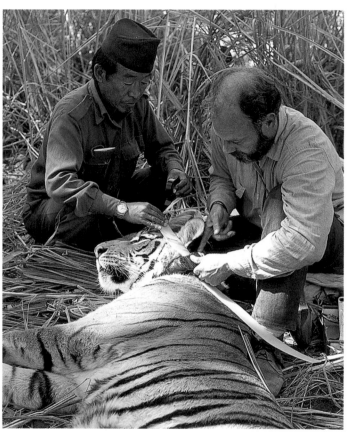

The Great Sphinx

In Egypt, an enormous statue with a human head and the body of a lion guards the Great Pyramids at Giza. This statue is the Great Sphinx. A story written in 1419 B.C. on the Sphinx tells of a prince named Thutmose IV who fell asleep between the paws of the statue. He dreamt that the Sun god told him to take away the sand covering part of the Sphinx and he would become a king. When he awoke, Thutmose did as he had been instructed, and the dream came true.

THE WORLD OF WILD DOGS

Wild dogs and wolves are powerful predators, hunting for prey in packs. They are sociable animals, living in highly organized groups, with individual members having their own role to play. Though often depicted in fairy stories as wicked, dangerous animals, they do not normally attack humans. Today more people appreciate their intelligence, loyalty and strong family ties – the same qualities that we value in our family pets.

What is a Wolf?

Wolves are wild members of the dog family, canids, with gleaming yellow eyes and lean, muscular bodies. The 37 different species of canids include wolves, jackals, coyotes, foxes and wild and domestic dogs. Canids are native to every continent except Australia and Antarctica. All of them share a keen sense of smell and hearing, and are carnivores (meat-eaters). Wolves and wild dogs hunt live prey, which they kill with their sharp teeth. However, many canids also eat vegetable matter and even insects. They are among the most intelligent of all animals. Some, such as wolves, are social in habit and live together in groups.

Large, triangular ears, usually held pricked (erect)

Powerful shoulders and supple body

▲ PRODUCING YOUNG

A female wolf suckles (feeds) her cubs. All canids are mammals and feed their young on milk. Females produce a litter of cubs, or pups, once a year. Most are born in an underground den.

BODY FEATURES ▶
The wolf is the largest wild dog. It has a strong, well-muscled body covered with dense, shaggy fur, a long, bushy tail and strong legs made for running. Its muzzle (nose and jaws) is long and well developed and its ears are pricked up. Male and female wolves look very similar, although females are generally the smaller of the two.

◄ KEEN SENSES

The jackal, like all dogs, has very keen senses. Its nose can detect faint scents and its large ears pick up the slightest sound. Smell and hearing are mainly used for hunting. Many canids also have good vision.

The Big, Bad Wolf
Fairy tales often depict wolves as wicked, dangerous animals. In the tale of the Three Little Pigs, the big, bad wolf terrorizes three small pigs. Eventually he is outwitted by the smartest pig, who builds a brick house that the wolf cannot blow down, and all the pigs are safe.

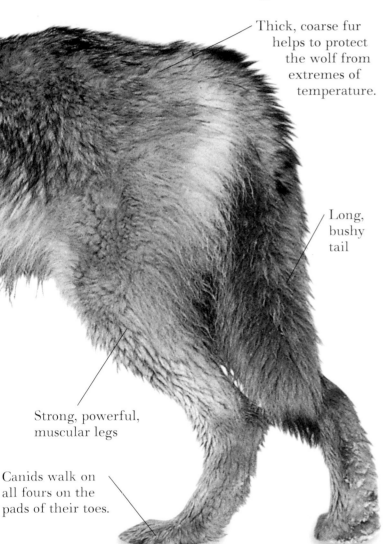

Thick, coarse fur helps to protect the wolf from extremes of temperature.

Long, bushy tail

Strong, powerful, muscular legs

Canids walk on all fours on the pads of their toes.

▲ LIVING IN PACKS

Wolves and a few other wild dogs live in groups called packs of about 8 to 20. Each pack has a hierarchy (social order) and is led by the strongest male and female.

EXPERT HUNTERS ►

A wolf bares its teeth in a snarl to defend its kill. Wolves and other canids feed mainly on meat, but eat plants, too, particularly when they are hungry.

The Wolf Family

Wolves were once common throughout the northern hemisphere, right across North America, Europe and Asia. In the past, people hunted them mercilessly. In many areas they died out altogether. Across the north, wolves from various regions may look quite different, but they are all one species, *Canis lupus*. However, there are many subspecies (different types). Two of the main types are the gray wolf, also known as the timber wolf, and the Arctic, or tundra wolf. Many other subspecies are named after the area or habitat they come from, such as Mexican and steppe wolves. The same type of wolf may be known by different names in different areas. For example, the Arctic wolf is the same as the tundra wolf. The wolf's closest relatives are the coyote, the jackal, the dingo and the domestic dog.

▲ **NEARLY EXTINCT**
The red wolf (*Canis rufus*) is found only in the south-eastern U.S.A. It was once widespread, but became extinct in the wild. Today's red wolves stem from captive-bred wolves. They have longer legs and larger ears than the gray wolf and are named after the reddish fur on their heads, ears and legs. The gray wolf is thought to be a hybrid (cross) between the coyote and the wolf.

▼ **MOUNTAIN HOME**
The Simien wolf is found only in the Simien Mountains of Ethiopia, East Africa. It is about the same size as a coyote (3 ft long) and has a mainly reddish-brown coat, with pale fur on its belly and throat. The Simien wolf was once thought to be a kind of jackal. Now scientists have found out that it is a small wolf.

Did you know? Wolves kill prey animals as large as bison and as small as mice.

Simien wolf
(*Canis simensis*)

dingo
(*Canis*
familiaris)

◄ DOG WITHOUT BARK

The dingo lives in Australia
and Southeast Asia. It is now
wild, but its ancestors are
descended from tame dogs
that Aboriginal people brought
to the region from Asia more than
8,000 years ago. Dingoes are found
mainly in dry areas such as the
dusty Australian interior. They live
in small families, and sometimes
join other dingo families to hunt.

JACKAL ►

Jackals are found on the grassy plains
and in the woodlands of Africa,
southeastern Europe and southern Asia.
They live in pairs and stay with the same
mate for life. There are three species of jackal—side-
striped and black-backed jackals (found only in Africa)
and golden jackals.

black-backed jackal
(*Canis mesomelas*)

▲ COYOTE

The coyote (*Canis latrans*) is found
in North and Central America. It
mainly lives on prairies (grassy
plains) and in open woodlands and is
also known as the prairie or brush
wolf. Full-grown coyotes are half the
size of gray wolves. They live alone,
or in pairs and small family groups.

miniature
poodle
(*Canis*
familiaris)

◄ DOMESTIC DOG

You may not have seen
a wolf in the wild, but
you will know one of
its relatives, for all
domestic dogs are
descended from the
wolf. Dogs were the
first animals to be
tamed by people
over 12,000 years
ago. Now there are
over 400 breeds of
dog, including the
miniature poodle.

Wild Dogs

In addition to the wolf's immediate family, five species of wild dog are distantly related to wolves and to each other. Foxes are also canids but are not closely related to wild dogs or wolves. Of the wild dogs, the bush dog and maned wolf are both found in South America. The dhole and raccoon dog come from eastern Asia. The African hunting dog lives in central and southern Africa. Like other canids, the bodies of these animals are adapted to suit their way of life and their environment. Raccoon dogs and bush dogs are short-legged species that make their homes in underground burrows. Maned wolves and African hunting dogs have long legs to help them see over the long grass and scrub of savannas (grasslands) and woodlands. Human settlements are currently expanding in the areas where these wild dogs live and threatening their existence.

bush dog
(Speothos venaticus)

▲ **STURDY HUNTER**
The bush dog inhabits forests and marshes in Central and South America. It is stocky, with a brown coat and paler fur on its neck and head.

◄ **FOXY CORGI**
The dhole (*Cuon alpinus*) can be found in India and China, on the islands of Sumatra and Java, and also in parts of Russia. Adult dholes reach about 3 ft long, but have short legs. With their reddish coats, they look a little like Welsh Corgis with long, bushy tails. Dholes live in packs and do much of their hunting during the day.

Classification Chart

Kingdom	**Animalia**	all animals
Phylum	**Chordata**	animals with backbones
Class	**Mammalia**	hair-covered animals that feed their young on milk
Order	**Carnivora**	mammals that eat meat
Family	**Canidae**	all dogs
Genus	*Cuon*	
Species	*alpinus*	dhole

▲ CLASSIFICATION OF WILD DOGS

All wolves and wild dogs are canids (members of the dog family). Wolves and their close relatives belong to the genus (group) *Canis*, but the wild dogs shown here each belong to a different genus. The African hunting dog's scientific name (*Lycaon pictus*) is completely different from the dhole's (*Cuon alpinus*).

▲ MASKED HUNTER

The raccoon dog (*Nyctereutes procyonoides*) is found in eastern Europe, Siberia, China and Japan. Small in size, it reaches only 2 ft long and has a chunky build. Its summer coat is gray-brown, with darker eye patches like a raccoon's mask. Its winter coat is white. These dogs live alone or in small groups.

HAPPY IN A CROWD ▶

The African hunting dog lives on the grassy plains south of the Sahara Desert. This wild dog has a mottled coat, long legs and rounded ears. It grows to about 3½ ft long. African hunting dogs, like wolves, are social animals and live in packs. Males and females look very much alike and live to around the age of ten years old.

African hunting dog (*Lycaon pictus*)

◀ SHY LONER

The maned wolf (*Chrysocyon brachyurus*) lives in grasslands and swampy regions in eastern South America. Despite its name, this animal is not a wolf. Although its long legs have earned it the nickname "the fox on stilts," it is not a fox either. Maned wolves have mostly reddish fur with darker legs and a mane of long hair at the neck. They grow to about 4 ft long. Solitary and shy, maned wolves usually hunt at night.

71

Focus on

The skeletons of dogs buried with their owners in ancient tombs show that dogs have been domesticated for at least 12,000 years. All domestic dogs are descended from the wolf. The first dogs were probably bred from wolves tamed by hunters. These may have been captured as cubs and brought back to camp to help with hunting. Later, ancient peoples began to develop different breeds of dogs by selecting animals with definite features that they valued. From these beginnings developed the 400 different breeds we know today. Domestic dogs come in an amazing variety of shapes and sizes, from the tiny chihuahua to the huge St. Bernard. Modern breeders divide the breeds into six main families: hounds, sporting dogs, working dogs, terriers, toys and utility (useful) dogs.

ANCIENT BREED
The pharaoh hound is one of the world's oldest dog breeds. It was produced in Egypt around 4,000 years ago as a swift hunting dog. Other breeds, such as the fierce mastiff, were developed as guard dogs. By Roman times, around 500 B.C., many of the breeds we know today had already been developed.

WORKING DOG
Border collies are working dogs and are used to herd sheep. The Border collie came from the Borders, an area on either side of the boundaries of England and Scotland. Working dogs have been bred to perform many useful tasks, from guarding homes to pulling sledges. This group includes corgis, boxers, mastiffs and huskies.

Domestic Dogs

BRED TO FETCH AND CARRY

A golden retriever fetches a duck shot by its owner. Retrievers, setters, spaniels and pointers are all sporting dogs, bred to help with hunting game birds. These naturally reliable and obedient dogs make good pets.

SPEEDY DOG

A greyhound's body is built for speed, with long legs, a flexible back and small, pointed head. It is bred in many countries for racing. People have bred racing dogs for centuries. In the past, dogs were often bred for cruel sports such as bear-baiting. Today these sports are against the law in many countries.

BURROWING EXPERT

The wire-haired fox terrier was very popular in England during the 1800s. The name terrier comes from the Latin *terra* (earth). All terriers were bred to hunt animals in burrows, such as foxes, rabbits, rats and badgers.

HUNTING HOUNDS

A pack of foxhounds follow the scent of their quarry, a fox. Various breeds of hound have been developed to hunt different animals, including wolves, deer, rabbits, badgers and foxes. Foxhounds, beagles and bloodhounds track their prey by scent. Wolfhounds were bred to hunt wolves and deer. Afghan hounds were bred to chase antelope (similar to deer) and hunt by sight.

Body Shapes

Like all mammals, wolves and dogs are vertebrates (animals with backbones). The backbone protects the spinal cord, the main nerve of the body. The bones in the skeleton support the body and give it a distinct shape. The skeletons of wolves and dogs are different from other mammals. They have long skulls with large teeth, longish necks, and long, strong leg bones. Narrow collar bones help to make them slim and streamlined for speed over the ground, while their joints at the shoulders and hips pivot freely, giving them great agility. Wolves, foxes and wild dogs also generally have long tails. Many have a well-defined tail shape that can help to identify the animal at a distance.

Backbone (spine)

Tail bones

Toe bones

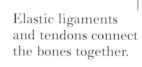
Elastic ligaments and tendons connect the bones together.

▲ **TALL AND GRACEFUL**

The maned wolf has longer leg bones than a true wolf. It uses them to hunt in the tall grass of its homeland. Its leg bones are weaker than a wolf's so it often lacks the power and strength to run down swift-moving prey. It has a short tail.

▲ **BUILT FOR POUNCING**

A fox's skeleton looks small and delicate compared to a wolf's. The leg bones are shorter in relation to its body size. Foxes spend much of their lives crouching and slinking through the undergrowth rather than running down prey.

74

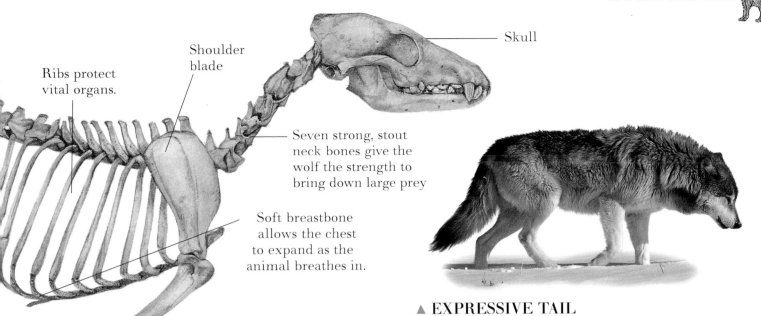

Skull

Shoulder blade

Ribs protect vital organs.

Seven strong, stout neck bones give the wolf the strength to bring down large prey

Soft breastbone allows the chest to expand as the animal breathes in.

Elbow joint

◀ STRONG AND FAST

Wolves are the largest of all canids apart from the biggest breeds of domestic dog. Wolves grow up to 6 ft long and weigh up to 175 lbs. Their streamlined bodies are built for fast running. Strong leg bones make the wolf a tireless hunter.

▲ EXPRESSIVE TAIL

The wolf holds its tail in different positions to express its feelings and show its position in the pack. Its bushy tail grows up to 1½ ft long.

▲ BALANCING BRUSH

The red fox's tail, known as a brush, is long and bushy. It grows up to 1½ ft long and helps to balance the animal when running and jumping.

Strong Like the Wolf

Native Americans admired the strength, courage and intelligence of wolves and wild dogs. Plains tribes such as the Blackfoot and Mandan formed warrior-bands called Dog Societies to honor the loyalty shown by wild dogs to other dogs in their pack. This Hidatsa shaman (medicine man) is dressed for the Dog Dance. Dances were performed in celebration and for good luck.

▲ TAIL TALK

The African hunting dog's tail is short compared to most canids, about 1–1½ ft long. Its white tip stands out clearly and is used to signal other members of the pack.

Body Parts

Muscular, fast-running wolves and wild dogs are built for chasing prey in open country. Thick muscles and long, strong legs enable them to run fast over great distances. The long skull helps the wolf to seize prey on the run. The wolf has a large stomach that can digest meat quickly and hold a big meal after a successful hunt. Wolves, however, can also go without food for more than a week if prey is scarce. Teeth are a wolf's main weapon, used for biting enemies, catching prey and tearing food. Small incisors (front teeth) strip flesh off bones. Long fangs (canines) grab and hold prey. Towards the back, jagged carnassial teeth close together like shears to chew meat into small pieces, while large molars can crush bones.

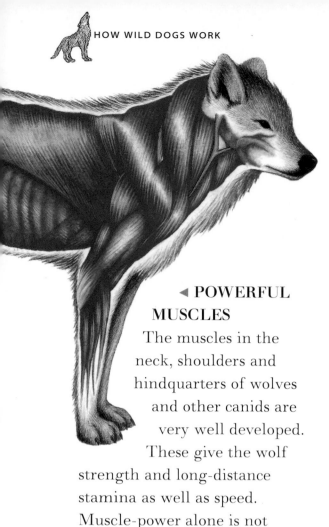

◄ **POWERFUL MUSCLES**
The muscles in the neck, shoulders and hindquarters of wolves and other canids are very well developed. These give the wolf strength and long-distance stamina as well as speed. Muscle-power alone is not enough, however, to catch prey. Wolves also need to use their cunning and stealth if the hunt is to succeed.

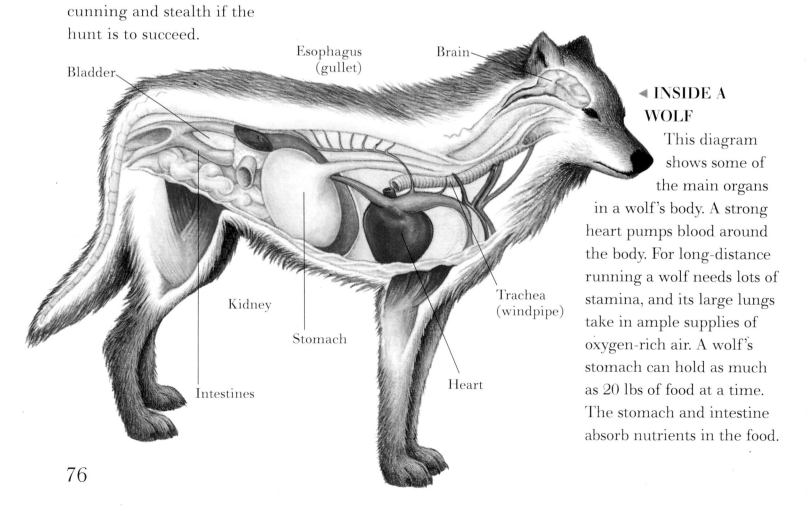

Bladder

Esophagus (gullet)

Brain

Kidney

Stomach

Intestines

Heart

Trachea (windpipe)

◄ **INSIDE A WOLF**
This diagram shows some of the main organs in a wolf's body. A strong heart pumps blood around the body. For long-distance running a wolf needs lots of stamina, and its large lungs take in ample supplies of oxygen-rich air. A wolf's stomach can hold as much as 20 lbs of food at a time. The stomach and intestine absorb nutrients in the food.

▼ WOLF'S SKULL

A wolf's head has a broad crown and a tapering muzzle. The bones of the skull are strong and heavy. They form a tough case that protects the animal's brain, eyes, ears and nose. The jaws have powerful muscles that can exert great pressure as the wolf sinks its teeth in its prey.

Molar   Carnassial   Canine   Incisor

▼ BAT-EARED FOX SKULL

The bat-eared fox has a delicate, tapering muzzle. Its jaws are weaker than a wolf's and suited to deal with smaller prey, such as insects. This fox has 46–50 teeth, which is more than any other canid. Extra molars at the back of the animal's mouth enable it to crunch insects, such as beetles, which have a tough outer casing on their bodies.

Molar   Carnassial   Canine   Incisor

▲ TIME FOR BED

A wolf shows its full set of meat-eating teeth as it yawns. Wolves and most other canids have 42 teeth. In wolves, the four large, dagger-like canines at the front of the mouth can grow up to 2 in. long.

COOLING DOWN ▶

Like all mammals, the wolf is warm-blooded. This means its body temperature remains constant whatever the weather, so it is always ready to spring into action. Wolves do not have sweat glands all over their bodies as humans do, so in hot weather they cannot sweat to cool down. When the wolf gets too hot, it opens its mouth and pants with its large tongue lolling out. Moisture evaporates from the nose, mouth and tongue to cool the animal down.

On the Move

Wolves are tireless runners. They can lope along for hours on end at a steady pace of 25 mph without resting. They have been known to cover an amazing 125 miles in a day searching for food. Compared to cheetahs, which can reach speeds of 55 mph over short distances, wolves are not fast runners. They can, however, put on a burst of speed to overtake fleeing prey.

Wolves and most other canids have four toes on their back feet and five toes on their front feet. The fifth toe on the front foot is called the dew claw, a small, functionless claw located a little way up on each front leg. They are more like pads than claws. They also have tough pads on the underside of their toes to help absorb the impact shock as the wolf's feet hit the ground.

▲ SPEEDING COYOTE

Like wolves, coyotes are good long-distance runners. They run on their toes, like all canids. This helps them to take long strides and so cover more ground. If necessary, coyotes can trot along for hours in search of food.

Did you know? Studies of wolves in the U.S. show one pack traveled 700 mi. in 40 days.

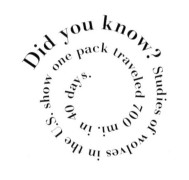

◀ IN MID-LEAP
Strong leg muscles enable a wolf to leap long distances—up to 15 ft in a single bound. Wolves and other canids are very agile and can leap upward, sideways and even backward. As the wolf lands, its toes splay out to support its weight and prevent it from slipping.

gray wolf
(*Canis lupus*)

Ankle joint

Bones in the foreleg are fused together.

Toe bone

LONG TOE ▶

This close-up of the bones in a maned wolf's foreleg shows the long toe bones that are used for walking. The bones in the foreleg, after the ankle joint and before the toes, are fused together for greater strength. Of all the canids, only the African hunting dog does not have dew claws.

▲ WOLF TRACK

Clawmarks show up clearly in a line of wolf prints in a snowy landscape. Unlike cats, wolves and wild dogs cannot retract (draw in) their claws. When walking, the wolf places its paws almost in a straight line, to form a single track. The pawprints of a running wolf are more widely spaced.

IN THE WATER ▶

Bush dogs make their homes near streams and rivers and spend much of their lives in water. They are strong swimmers, and water creatures such as capybaras (a type of rodent) form part of their diet. Wolves, dingoes and most other canids can also swim well.

A KEEN CLIMBER ▶

Wolves and wild dogs are quick on the ground, but they cannot climb trees. Some foxes, however, climb well. The gray fox of North America is an expert climber. It scrambles up trees to steal birds' eggs and chicks. It also climbs to get a good view over surrounding countryside when searching for prey.

gray fox
(*Urocyon cinereoargenteus*)

79

Fur Coats

black-backed jackal
(Canis mesomelas)

Wolves and other members of the dog family have thick fur coats. This dense layer of hair helps to protect the animal's body from injury and keeps it warm in cold weather. Wolves and other canids that live in cold places have extra-thick fur. Dingoes, jackals and wild dogs that live in warm countries close to the equator have sparser fur. The fur is made up of two layers. Short dense underfur helps to keep the animal warm. Long guard hairs on top have natural oils that repel snow and rain to keep the underfur dry. A wild dog's fur coat is usually black, white or tan, or a mixture of these colors. Markings and patterns on the fur act as camouflage to disguise these animals, so they can sneak up unseen on their prey.

▲ JACKAL COLORS
The three species of jackal can be distinguished by their different markings. As its name suggests, the black-backed jackal has a dark patch on its back as well as brown flanks and a pale belly. The golden jackal is sandy brown all over. The side-striped jackal is so named because of the light and dark stripes that run along its sides.

◄ WAITING FOR SPRING
Two raccoon dogs shelter under a bush waiting for the snow to melt. They already have their summer coats of gray with pale and dark patches. This will help to camouflage them among the summer grasses and vegetation. In autumn, they will molt (shed) these coats and grow a pure-white coat, ready for the winter snow.

◄ MANES AND RUFFS

The maned wolf gets its name from the ruff of long hairs on its neck. This may be dark or reddish brown in color. Wolves also have a ruff of longer hairs that they raise when threatened to make themselves look larger.

▲ HANDSOME CAMOUFLAGE

African hunting dogs have beautiful markings, with tan and dark gray patches on their bodies, and paler, mottled fur on their heads and legs. The patterns work to break up the outline of their bodies as they hunt in the dappled light of the bush.

Arctic wolf
(Canis lupus tundarum)

▲ WARM COAT

The Arctic wolf has very thick fur to keep it warm in icy temperatures. Its winter coat is pure white so that it blends in with the snow. In spring, the thick fur drops out and the wolf grows a thinner coat for summer. This coat is usually darker to match the earth without its covering of snow.

VARYING COLORS ►

Gray wolves vary greatly in color, from pale silver to buff, sandy, red-brown or almost black. Even very dark wolves usually have some pale fur, often a white patch on the chest.

gray wolf
(Canis lupus)

Smell, Touch and Taste

Of all the senses, smell is the most important for wolves and wild dogs. These animals are constantly surrounded by different scents and their keen sense of smell can distinguish them all. They follow the scent trails left behind by other animals in their quest for food, and can pick up even faint whiffs of scent on the wind. This helps them to figure out the direction of distant prey. Canids that hunt in packs use scent to identify and communicate with other pack members. They also communicate by sight and touch.

Like other mammals, wolves and wild dogs have taste buds on their tongues to taste their food. They eat foods they find the tastiest first. The tongue is also used to lap up water.

▲ **TRACKING PREY**

Nose to the ground, a wolf follows a scent trail in the snow. From the scent a wolf can tell what type of animal left it, whether it is well or ill, how far away it is and whether another wolf is following the trail.

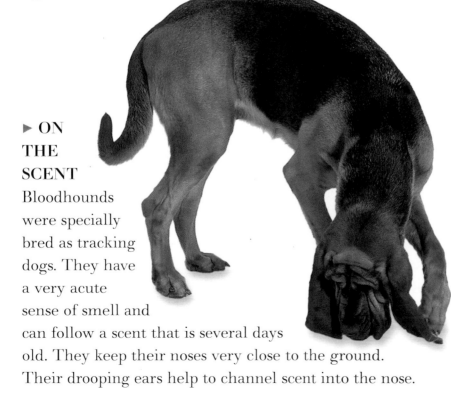

▶ **ON THE SCENT**

Bloodhounds were specially bred as tracking dogs. They have a very acute sense of smell and can follow a scent that is several days old. They keep their noses very close to the ground. Their drooping ears help to channel scent into the nose.

▲ **PLEASED TO MEET YOU**

When two wolves meet they sniff the glands at the base of the tail. Pack members all have a familiar scent. Scent is also used to signal mood, such as contentment or fear, or if a female is ready to breed.

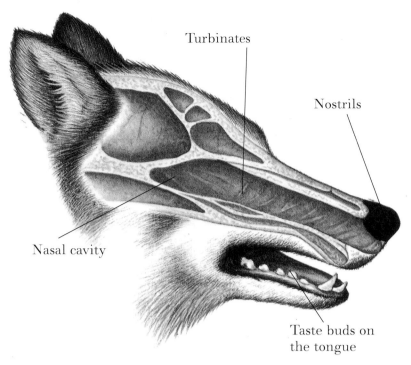

Turbinates

Nostrils

Nasal cavity

Taste buds on
the tongue

▲ INSIDE THE SNOUT

Inside a wolf's snout is a large nasal cavity used
for smelling. Scent particles pass over tubes of
very thin bone in the roof of the nasal cavity.
These tubes, called turbinates, are connected to
a nerve network that sends signals to the brain.

▼ SENSITIVE NOSE

The wolf's leathery outer nose is set
right at the end of
its snout. Two
nostrils draw air
laden with scents into
the nasal cavity. The
wolf may flare its
nostrils to take in extra
air. The animal may
lick its nose before
scenting, because a
damp nose helps its
sense of smell. Long,
sensitive whiskers on
either side of the
snout are used for
touching things
at close range.

▲ TOUCHY-FEELY

Wolves use touch to bond with each other.
They rub bodies, lick one another and thrust
their noses into each other's fur when they
meet. Pack members play-fight by wrestling
with locked jaws, or chasing around in circles.

▲ WELL GROOMED

A wolf nibbles at the tufts of hair
between its paw pads. It is
removing ice that might cut and
damage the paw. Wolves groom
(clean) their fur to keep it in good
condition. Licking and running
fur through the teeth helps to
remove dirt and dislodge fleas.

85

Living Together

Wolves are very social animals. A few may live alone, but most live in packs. A wolf pack may contain as few as 2 or as many as 36 animals. Most packs have between 8 and 24 members. The main purpose of the pack is to hunt. A team of wolves working together can hunt down and kill much larger and stronger prey than a wolf would be able to on its own. Only the strongest, healthiest pair in the wolf pack will actually mate. Every pack member then helps to feed and bring up the cubs. Bush dogs, dholes and African hunting dogs also live in packs, while jackals, and sometimes coyotes and raccoon dogs, live in smaller family groups. Maned wolves and foxes usually live alone.

▲ **TWO'S COMPANY**

A pair of jackals drinks from a water hole in South Africa. Some jackals are solitary, but most pair up for life. The cubs are reared in small, close-knit family groups. Older brothers or sisters often help their parents to rear the small cubs.

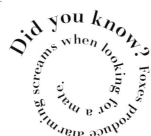

Did you know? Foxes produce alarming screams when looking for a mate.

WOLF PACK ▶

A wolf pack is led by the strongest, most experienced animals. The rest of the pack often consists of their children—young cubs and older, half-grown wolves. The young wolves follow their leaders until they are old enough to leave the pack.

maned wolf
(*Chrysocyon brachyurus*)

▲ A FAMILY AFFAIR

Dholes live in family packs of between 5 and 12 animals. Sometimes several families join together to form a very large dhole pack called a clan. Hunting in a big group helps these relatively small wild dogs to tackle large prey such as wild cattle and buffalo.

▲ EACH FOR ITSELF

The maned wolf is mostly solitary, living and hunting on its own. Males and females pair up during the breeding season. The male helps to feed and rear his pups—as do all canids, except for the domestic dog.

◄ COYOTE COUPLE

Most coyotes live and hunt alone, in pairs or in small family units. Sometimes, several of these small groups band together to make a bigger hunting party to go after large prey.

DOG SOCIETY ▶

African hunting dogs are the next most social canids after wolves. They hunt cooperatively and all pack members help to raise the pups of the breeding pair. The males in the pack are all brothers. Females often join from different packs.

Focus on

A wolf pack has a strict social order and each member knows its place. The senior male and female, known as the alpha male and female, are the only animals to breed. The alpha male takes the lead in hunting, defends the pack members from enemies, and keeps the other animals in their place. In most packs, a second pair of wolves, called the beta male and female, come next in the ranking order. The other pack members are usually the offspring of the alpha pair, aged up to three years old.

LEADER OF THE PACK

An alpha male wolf greets a junior pack member. Wolves use different body positions and facial expressions to show rank. The leader stands upright with tail held high. The junior has his ears laid back and his tail tucked between his legs.

IT'S A PUSHOVER

A junior wolf rolls over on its back in a gesture of submission to a more dominant pack member. A junior wolf can also pacify a stronger animal by imitating cub behavior, such as begging for food.

SHOWING WHO IS BOSS

A wolf crouches down to an alpha male. The young wolf whines as it cowers, as if to say, "You're the boss." The pack leader's confident stance makes him look as large as possible.

a Wolf Pack

"I GIVE UP"

A male gray wolf lays its ears back and sticks its tongue out. Taken together, these two gestures signal submission. A wolf with its tongue out, but its ears pricked, is sending a different message, showing it feels hostile and rebellious.

REJECTED BY THE PACK

Old, wounded or sickly wolves are often turned out of the pack to become lone wolves. Although pack members may be affectionate with each other, there is no room for sentiment. Young wolves may also leave to start their own packs. Lone wolves without the protection of a pack are much more vulnerable to attack and must be more cautious.

SCARY SNARL

A gray wolf bares its canine teeth in a snarl of aggression. Studies have shown that wolves use up to 20 different facial expressions. Junior wolves use snarling expressions to challenge the authority of their leaders. The alpha male may respond with an even more ferocious snarl. If it does so, the junior wolf is faced with a choice. It must back down, or risk being punished with a nip.

89

Home Territory

▲ KEEP TO THE TRAIL

A pack of wolves runs along a snowy trail in single file. Each wolf treads in the tracks of the one in front. This saves a lot of energy that would be wasted if each animal broke a separate trail through the deep snow. Wolves use well-worn paths inside their territories. These connect meeting places with lookout points and good ambush sites.

Territories are areas that animals use for finding food or for breeding. An animal will defend its territory against others that might provide competition. Wolf packs use their territories as hunting grounds and also as safe places to raise their cubs. Wolf territories vary in size, depending on how much food is available to feed the pack. Small territories cover about 65 square miles. Large territories may be 10 or even 100 times this size. At the heart of the territory is the rendezvous, a meeting place where the wolves gather. This place also acts as a nursery where older cubs are left to play. The borders of the territory are patrolled by the pack on a regular basis, and marked with urine. Strong-smelling urine sprayed at marker sites lasts several days, while howling also serves as a long-distance warning. The pack will defend its territory fiercely if a rival pack tries to enter.

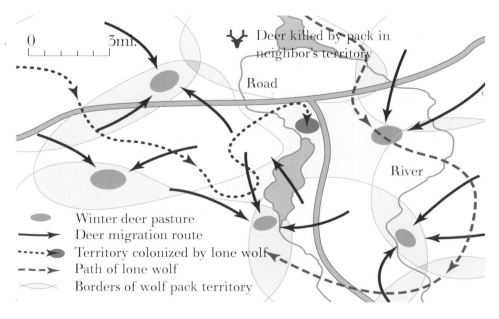

0   3mi.

Deer killed by pack in
neighbor's territory

Road

River

Winter deer pasture
Deer migration route
Territory colonized by lone wolf
Path of lone wolf
Borders of wolf pack territory

◄ NEIGHBORING TERRITORIES

Several wolf territories may lie close to each other. Where food is plentiful, for example where deer breed, territories may overlap (see diagram). Rivers, towns and roads form natural boundaries. There may be a neutral ½-mile wide no-go area between territories. If food becomes scarce, however, wolves will enter this zone.

▲ SCENT SIGNAL

A wolf smells a rock that another pack member has marked with urine. The scent lingers for several days after the animal has moved on. A wolf smelling this signal can tell how many animals have passed this way and whether they belong to its pack. Wolves from a rival pack will mark the other side of the rock to reinforce territory boundaries.

▲ BORDER DISPUTE

A wolf snarls at a wolf from another pack on the boundary between their territories. When food is scarce, packs are more likely to trespass or raid each other's territory. In times of plenty, scent signals keep trespassers out, so border disputes are rare.

◄ SCENT-MARKING

A dhole marks the edge of its territory by spraying urine on a patch of grass. Some canids, such as African hunting dogs and foxes, leave piles of droppings too. In a wolf pack, it is usually the alpha male that marks the boundaries.

KEEP-OUT CALL ►

Three wolves raise their heads in a group howl. Each animal howls a slightly different note, making an eerie harmony. The sound carries over a long distance—6 mi. or more. If it reaches a rival pack, the other wolves may howl back. Howling is also used to rally the pack, for example, before a hunt.

A Meaty Diet

Wolves and their relatives are carnivores (meat-eaters). They kill prey for fresh meat, but also eat carrion (dead animals). When no meat is available wolves eat plants, such as fruit and berries, and also grass to aid digestion. Large herd animals such as musk oxen, moose, deer and caribou are the favorite targets of the wolf pack. All canids target other kinds of prey if a particular creature becomes scarce. For example, they hunt a wide range of smaller animals, including birds, rabbits, mice and beavers.

Wolves swim well and chase fish, frogs and crabs, but still spend much of their lives with empty bellies. When food is scarce, they sometimes approach towns and villages, where they riffle through rubbish or kill domestic sheep, goats, cattle and horses.

▲ NOT-SO-FUSSY FEEDERS

Raccoon dogs of eastern Asia are omnivores—they eat all kinds of different foods, including rodents, fruit and acorns. They are strong swimmers and catch frogs, fish and water beetles in streams and rivers. They also scavenge carrion and scraps from people's garbage cans.

▼ COYOTE PREY

Three coyotes tear at the carcass of a moose. Coyotes usually hunt small prey such as mice, but sometimes they band together to go after larger creatures such as moose. Teams of coyotes also gang up on other predators and steal their kills.

◄ FAST FOOD

A pack of dholes works quickly to eat the deer carcass. Each one eats fast to get its share. A hungry dhole can eat up to 10 lbs of meat in an hour. Mammals form a large part of a dhole's diet, but if meat is scarce a dhole will also eat berries, lizards and insects.

▲ MEAT AND FRUIT-EATER

A maned wolf lopes off in search of prey. Without a pack to help it hunt, it looks for easy prey, including armadillos and small rodents such as agoutis and pacas. It also feeds on birds, reptiles, frogs and insects, fruit and sugar cane.

▲ BEACH SQUABBLE

Two black-backed jackals squabble over the carcass of a seal pup. Jackals eat almost anything—fruit, frogs, reptiles and a wide range of mammals, from gazelles to mice. Jackals also scavenge kills from other hunters.

CACHING FOOD ►

A wolf looks for a suitable spot in the snow to bury a freshly caught rabbit. After a pack has killed a large beast, or when a lone hunter has eaten its fill, it hides the remains of its food. Then, when food is scarce, the wolf can return to the hidden cache and retrieve its kill.

Did you know? All canids are quick feeders, but dholes in particular consume their food at a great rate.

gray wolf
(*Canis lupus*)

Going Hunting

Wolves and wild dogs do not all hunt at the same time of day. Maned wolves, bush dogs and raccoon dogs are mainly nocturnal (active at night). They rely on smell and hearing to find their prey. Dholes and African hunting dogs are daytime hunters, and track their prey by sight as well as smell and sound. Wolves hunt at any time of day or night. Members of a wolf pack work together like players in a sports team. Each animal has particular strengths that help the group. Some wolves are good trackers, others are particularly cunning, fast, or powerful, and so help to bring down large animals such as moose. Wolves spend a lot of time searching for food. A hunt may last for several hours, but nine out of ten hunts are unsuccessful and the wolves go hungry. If they strike lucky, they might kill a beast large enough to provide meat for all the pack.

Little Red Riding Hood
In the story of Little Red Riding Hood, a cunning wolf eats Red Riding Hood's grandmother. The wolf then steals the old woman's clothes to prey on the little girl. Fortunately a wood cutter rescues Red Riding Hood in the nick of time. As he kills the wolf, the grandmother emerges alive from inside the wolf.

◀ WOLF PACK IN ACTION
Wolves use skill as well as strength to hunt large creatures such as moose. A moose calf is an easier target than a full-grown animal. The wolves stalk their prey, fanning out and running ahead to surround the victim. Pack members dash forward to panic the animals and separate the mother from her baby. Once the young calf is separated, the wolves run it down and kill it with a bite to the neck.

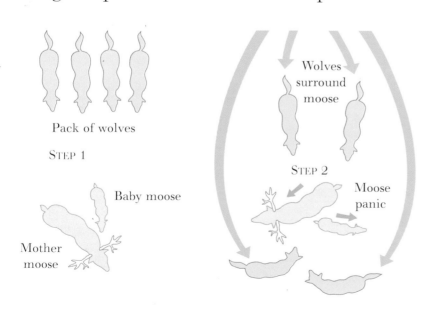

Pack of wolves

STEP 1

Baby moose

Mother moose

Wolves surround moose

STEP 2

Moose panic

DINGO KILL ▶

Two dingoes have just caught a kangaroo. In the Australian outback, dingoes hunt a wide range of creatures, from tiny grasshoppers and lizards to large prey such as wild pigs and kangaroos. Sheep, introduced by settlers in the 1800s, are a favorite target.

◀ GROUP KILL

A large pack of wolves has killed a white-tailed deer. This amount of meat will not satisfy the group for long. Where food is scarce, territories are often much larger than in places where the hunting is easy. The pack will always hunt the largest game it can find.

Did you know For peak condition, a wolf needs to eat 9 lbs of meat a day.

coyote
(Canis latrans)

CLEVER TACTICS ▶

A coyote plays with a mouse it has surprised in the snow. Coyotes often hunt

mice, leaping high in the air to pounce on their victims. Coyotes have a more varied diet than wolves, feeding on fruit, grass, berries and insects, as well as mammals such as rabbits, deer and rodents. They catch fish and frogs in the water, and also steal sheep and chickens, which makes them unpopular with farmers.

▲ TEAMWORK

Working as a team, dholes hunt large prey such as sambar (a type of deer). Dholes whistle to keep in touch with one another as they surround their prey. Teamwork also helps the pack to defend the kill from scavengers such as vultures.

95

Focus on African

African hunting dogs eat more meat than any other canid. One in every three of their hunts ends in a kill, a very high success rate. They live on the savanna (grassy plains) of central and southern Africa, which is also home to vast herds of grazing animals such as zebra, wildebeest and gazelle. The pack wanders freely over a huge area of savanna, looking for herd animals to prey on. They rely on sight to find their quarry, so they hunt during daylight hours or on bright moonlit nights. They mainly hunt at dusk or dawn when the air is coolest and rest in the shade during the hottest time of day.

1 A pack of wild dogs begins to run down their quarry, a powerful wildebeest. On the open plains of the Serengeti in East Africa, there is little cover that would allow the dogs to sneak up on their prey. The hunt is often therefore a straightforward chase. A junior dog may lead the hunt at first. The pack also targets many kinds of antelope, such as kudu and gazelle.

2 The dogs run along at an easy lope at first. They have tested out the wildebeest herd to find an easy target. They look for weak, injured, or young and inexperienced animals that will make suitable victims. This wildebeest is an older animal whose strength may be failing.

Hunting Dogs

3 A hunting dog tries to seize the wildebeest's tail. Hunting dogs with different strengths and skills take on different roles during the hunt. The lead dogs are in excellent condition and strong. They dodge out of the way if the wildebeest turns to defend itself with its sharp hooves and horns. Fast runners spread out to surround the victim and cut off its escape.

4 As the wildebeest tires, two dogs grip its snout and tail, pinning it down. Hunting dogs can run at 30 mph for quite a distance, but their prey is much quicker. While the lead dogs follow the fleeing animal's twists and turns, backmarkers take a more direct line, saving their strength. The rear dogs take over the chase as the leaders tire.

5 More dogs arrive and the strongest move in for the kill. While some dogs hold their victim by the snout and flanks, others jump up to knock it off balance. The dogs attack their victim's sides and rump and soon the animal is bleeding freely. It begins to weaken through shock and loss of blood.

6 The wildebeest crashes to the ground and the dogs rip at its underparts to kill it. There is little snapping and snarling as they eat, but the kill is fiercely defended if a scavenger such as a jackal comes close. Half-grown cubs feed first, then the carcass is ripped apart and bones, skin and all are eaten. Back at the den young cubs are fed with pre-chewed meat.

Finding a Mate

Wolves and wild dogs breed once a year, toward the end of winter. The cubs are born roughly two months later, in the spring. The size of the litter varies from species to species. Maned wolves give birth to the fewest young, usually only two cubs. Each pregnant wolf produces between three and eight cubs per litter. African hunting dogs have the largest litters—up to 16 pups at a time.

About six weeks after mating, a female wolf prepares a den in a cave, a hollow tree trunk or an underground burrow. Here her cubs will be born. The pack gathers outside the den as she begins to give birth. They howl as if to encourage the mother as the young are born.

▲ PURE PEDIGREE

In some parts of Australia, dingoes live in packs, in which only the dominant female breeds. In other areas, they live in smaller family groups. Because there are no other wild dogs to breed with, dingoes are in fact the most pure bred dogs in the world. They are directly descended from prehistoric domestic dogs.

Did you know? Wolf cubs take about 63 days to develop in their mother's womb before they are born.

COURTING COUPLE ▶

A male wolf sniffs his partner to find out if she is ready to mate. Tensions run high in the wolf pack during the breeding season, as all the adult wolves are ready to breed. The alpha male and female must dominate the rest to make sure they are the only ones to mate. The alpha female temporarily drives the other females from the pack. Once the alpha pair have mated, all the wolves can relax.

◄ MATING WOLVES

When they mate, the male wolf mounts the female and grasps her sides with his front paws. The female becomes ready to mate as the periods of daylight grow longer. This means that her pups will be born in spring as the weather warms up and food becomes plentiful. In North America, in the south of their range, if mating is in February the cubs will be born in late April or May. Farther north, wolves give birth in May or June.

LOCKED TOGETHER ►

Directly after mating, canids often stay tied (locked together) for many minutes. Tying helps to ensure that the alpha male is the father of the cubs, rather than an alpha male from a rival pack that may mate with the alpha female afterward. It also helps strengthen the bond between parent wolves.

◄ DINGO DEN

A rocky cave overlooking a stony desert makes a good den site for this mother dingo. The cave will be a safe, cool and shady place for the cubs to be born.

▲ GIVING BIRTH

A mother wolf licks her newborn cub to clean it and stimulate it to begin breathing. Wolf cubs are born at intervals of about 15 to 30 minutes, and it may take up to six hours for a large litter to be born.

99

Newborn Cubs

At birth the young of wolves and dogs are tiny and helpless. Newborn wolves are only about 8 inches long from the tip of their short noses to the end of their thin, little tails. With eyes tightly closed, they cannot see or hear, or even stand on their weak legs. They squirm around and huddle close to their mother for warmth. Like all mammals, their first food is their mother's rich milk, which she encourages them to suck from the moment they are born.

After one or two weeks, the cubs' eyes open and they take notice of their surroundings. They take their first wobbly steps and scramble over each other in the den. At about five weeks, the cubs begin to take solid food as well as milk. Half-chewed meat, stored in the stomach of an adult wolf, is brought to the den and regurgitated when the cubs beg for food.

▲ **AT THE DEN**

Wolf cubs take a first look at the big world outside their den. For nearly eight weeks their only experience has been the burrow—a 15-ft-long tunnel dug in soft earth with room for an adult wolf to creep along. The cubs sleep in a cozy chamber at the end, while their mother sleeps in a hollow nearer the entrance.

Did you know? Young wolf cubs need to feed every few hours and drink 10 oz of milk a day.

NURSING MOTHER ►

The mother wolf hardly leaves her cubs for the first weeks of their lives. Her mate, and the other members of the pack, bring food so she does not need to leave the den to go hunting. As a nursing mother, she is always hungry and needs large quantities of food to produce enough milk to feed her hungry cubs.

▼ CUBS IN DANGER

These wolf cubs are about six or seven weeks old. Not all cubs are born in a den. Some are born in a hollow sheltered from the wind, or in a nest flattened in long grass. There are many dangers for cubs in the open. They may be snatched by predators such as bears or eagles. Many do not survive to adulthood.

gray wolf cubs
(*Canis lupus*)

Romulus and Remus
According to ancient Roman legend, Romulus and Remus were twin brothers who were abandoned as babies on a remote hillside. A she-wolf found them and brought them up, feeding them on her milk. Both brothers survived and Romulus went on to found the city of Rome.

▲ HUNGRY PUPPIES

An African hunting dog suckles her pups. They suck milk from two sets of nipples on her underside. Female hunting dogs often have more nipples than other canids, because they have the biggest litters and therefore the most mouths to feed. As the pups' sharp teeth begin to hurt she will wean them on meat.

▲ RARE CUBS

In the mountains of Ethiopia, a Simien wolf guards her litter of five cubs. Simien wolves have similar breeding habits to other wolves, but are much rarer. These cubs look healthy, so have a good chance of surviving long enough to breed as adults.

101

Growing Up

At eight weeks old, wolf cubs are very lively. Their snouts have grown longer, their ears stand up and they look much more like adult wolves. They run around on long, strong legs. Now weaned off milk, they live on a diet of meat brought by the adults. As they leave the safety of the den, the other pack members gather around and take great interest in the cubs. The cubs' new playground is the rendezvous, the safe place at the heart of wolf-pack territory where the adults gather. This is usually a sheltered, grassy spot near a stream where the cubs can drink. Here they develop their hunting skills by pouncing on mice and insects. In play-fights they establish a ranking order that mirrors the social order in the pack.

▲ CARRIED AWAY

A wolf carries a cub to safety by seizing the loose skin at the scruff of its neck in its teeth. This adult is most likely the cub's mother or father, but it may be another member of the pack. All the adult wolves are very tolerant with the youngsters to begin with. Later, as the cubs grow up, they may be punished with a well-placed nip if they are naughty.

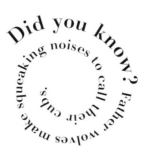

Did you know? Father wolves make squeaking noises to call their cubs.

SHARING A MEAL ▶

A young African hunting dog begs for food by whining, wagging its tail and licking the adult's mouth. The adult responds by arching its back and regurgitating (bringing up) a meal of half-digested meat from its stomach. The pups grow quickly on this diet. At the age of four months, they are strong enough to keep up with the pack when they go hunting.

▼ PRACTICE MAKES PERFECT

Two Arctic fox cubs practice their hunting skills by pouncing on one another. Wolf cubs play-fight to establish a ranking order. By the age of 12 weeks, one cub has managed to dominate the others. He or she may go on to become leader of a new pack.

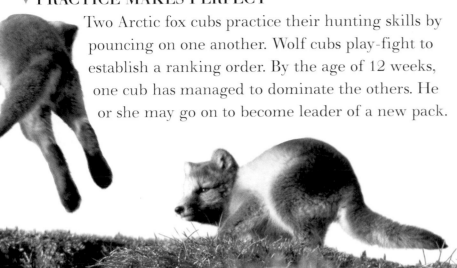

▲ YOUTHFUL CURIOSITY

Young maned wolves investigate their surroundings. Females usually bear three cubs at most. Newborn young have gray-brown fur, short legs and snouts. Later they develop long legs and handsome red fur.

Wolfchild

Rudyard Kipling's Jungle Book, *which was published in 1894, is set in India. The book tells the story of Mowgli, a young boy who is abandoned and brought up by wolves in the jungle. When Mowgli becomes a man he fights his archenemy, the tiger Shere Khan. Kipling's tale was inspired by many true-life accounts of wolf-children who grew up in the wild in India during the 1800s.*

ALMOST GROWN ▶

These two young wolves are almost full grown. Cubs can feed themselves at about ten months, but remain with the pack to learn hunting skills. At about two or three years old, many are turned out. They wander alone or with brothers or sisters until they find a mate and start a new pack.

Icy Wastes

Wolves were once widespread throughout the northern hemisphere. As human settlements have expanded, so wolves have been confined to more remote areas such as the far north. The Arctic is a frozen wilderness where very few people live. Wolves and Arctic foxes are found here. On the barren, treeless plains known as the tundra, harsh, freezing winter weather lasts for nine months of the year. Both land and sea are buried beneath a thick layer of snow and ice. Few animals are active in winter, so prey is scarce. During the brief summer, the ice and snow melt, flowers bloom and birds, insects and animals flourish, so prey is abundant. Arctic wolves and foxes rear their cubs in this time of plenty. Another harsh, remote habitat, the windswept grass steppes of Asia, is home to the small steppe wolf.

Arctic Legend
Native Americans named natural phenomena after the animals that lived around them. The Blackfoot called the Milky Way the Wolf Trail. In northern Canada, the Cree believed the Northern Lights, shown below, shone when heavenly wolves visited the Earth. In fact these spectacular light shows in the Arctic are caused by particles from the Sun striking the Earth's atmosphere.

Arctic wolf
(Canis lupus tundarum)

◄ **WHITE WOLF**
Arctic wolves are larger than most other wolf species. They scrape under the snow to nibble plant buds and lichen if they are desperate for food.

Did you know? *The largest Arctic wolf territories cover 5,000 square miles—more than half the size of Massachusetts.*

▲ WARM FUR

This Inuit girl is wearing a hood trimmed with wolf fur. The fur is warm and sheds the ice that forms on the hood's edge as the wearer breathes. The Inuit and other peoples of the far north traditionally dressed in the skins of Arctic animals. Animal skins make the warmest clothing and help to camouflage the wearer when hunting.

▲ ARCTIC HUNTER

A gray wolf feeds hungrily on a caribou carcass. In the icy north, wolves need very large territories to find enough prey. They will follow deer for hundreds of miles as the herds move south for the winter.

◀ ARCTIC HELPER

One crack of a whip brings a team of huskies under control. Tough and hardy huskies, with their thick fur coats, are the working dogs of the far north. They are used by the Inuit and other Arctic peoples to pull sleds and help to hunt.

SNOWY BED ▶

A gray wolf shelters in a snowy hollow to escape a howling blizzard. With its thick fur, it can sleep out in the open in temperatures as low as -25°F. Snow drifting over its body forms a protective blanket.

In the Forest

South of the treeless Arctic tundra, a belt of dense evergreen forests rings the northern hemisphere. It covers large parts of Canada, northern Europe and Russia. South of this belt lie the broad-leaved woodlands of temperate (warm) regions. Yet farther south, tropical rainforests grow in the hotter regions around the equator.

Wolves and other canids flourish in forests and woods where there is a plentiful supply of prey and dense undergrowth in which to hide and stalk. Wolves are perhaps most at home in temperate northern regions, where large game such as deer abound. In tropical rainforests, most creatures live high in the tree tops, where wild dogs cannot reach them. However, canids such as bush dogs and raccoon dogs are found near streams and rivers, which also teem with life.

▲ **WOODLAND JACKAL**
A side-striped jackal keeps a wary lookout for danger. In Africa, the three different kinds of jackal are found in different types of terrain. Side-striped jackals keep mostly to woods and swampy areas. Golden and black-backed jackals live in more open countryside.

◄ **HIDDEN HUNTERS**
In dark pine forests and dappled broad-leaved woodlands, the gray or blackish coats of wolves blend in with the shadows. This helps them to sneak up on deer, moose and other forest prey. Dense foliage also protects the wolves from the worst of the north's drenching rain.

◄ SOUND SLEEPERS

Raccoon dogs live in thickly wooded river valleys in eastern Asia. They are the only canids that hibernate in winter. In autumn raccoon dogs gorge themselves on fruit and meat to put on a thick layer of fat. Then they retreat to their burrows. They sleep right through the harsh winter and wake in spring.

raccoon dog
(Nyctereutes procyonoides)

JUNGLE PACK ►

A dhole moves through the thick undergrowth of a forest in India. Packs of dholes hunt deer such as chital and sambar. They call to one another to surround their prey as it moves through the dense jungle. The pack will guard its kills against bears, tigers and scavengers.

◄ RODENTS BEWARE

Bush dogs live in the dense forests and marshlands of South America. In the wetlands, their main prey are aquatic rodents such as pacas and agoutis. These fierce dogs will even plunge into the water to hunt capybaras— the world's largest rodents, 4 ft long.

Did you know? Raccoon dogs are the only canids that cannot bark.

A SCARCE BREED ►

A wolf surveys the snowy landscape in the Abruzzo region of central Italy. Wolves are common in remote forests in Canada and Russia, but in western Europe they are scarce. They survive in small pockets of wilderness, hiding in the hills by day and creeping down to villages to steal scraps at night.

Grassland and Desert

Grasslands are found on every continent except Antarctica. Savanna (grassland) is home to several canids, including maned wolves, black-backed jackals and African hunting dogs. Other canids, including coyotes, dingoes and several kinds of fox, live in deserts. In these harsh, barren places, the sun beats down mercilessly by day, but at night the temperature plummets. Scorching daytime temperatures may cause animals to overheat. Desert foxes keep cool during the hot days by hiding under shady rocks or in dark burrows, emerging to hunt only at night. Another big problem for desert animals is lack of water. Wild dogs and foxes can survive for long periods with little water, or derive most of the liquid they need from their food.

▲ DESERT WOLVES
Wolves are found in deserts and dry areas in Mexico, Iran and Arabia. With little vegetation to provide cover, they stalk prey by hiding behind boulders or rocky outcrops. Desert wolves often have pale or sandy fur, to blend in with their surroundings.

▲ GIVING OFF HEAT
A black-backed jackal's large ears contain a network of fine veins. Blood flowing through these veins gives off heat, keeping the animal cool.

◄ HUNTERS OF THE OUTBACK
A pair of dingoes waits at a rabbit warren in central Australia. Dingoes have lived wild in the outback for more than 8,000 years. Their reddish-brown coats, with paler fur on their legs and bellies, are perfect camouflage in the desert landscape.

▲ OUTCAST DOGS

Feral dogs are the descendants of domestic dogs that have become wild. In Asia they are known as pariah (outcast) dogs. Feral dogs are very adaptable and change their behavior to suit any situation. In India, pariah dogs hang around villages and sneak in to scavenge scraps.

▲ SMALLER PACKS

A pack of African hunting dogs tears a carcass apart. In the past, hunting dogs were numerous and widespread throughout central and southern Africa. Packs were large, containing 100 animals or more. Now these wild dogs are much more scarce and their packs are also smaller, usually containing between 6 and 30 animals.

▲ SLY HUNTER

A maned wolf hunts in the long grass in Argentinian marshland. Despite its long legs, this canid is not a fast runner. It also lacks the stamina needed to chase prey over great distances. Instead, it stalks animals such as rodents by slowly sneaking up on them before making a sudden pounce.

The Jackal-headed God

In ancient Egypt, Anubis, the god of the dead, was shown with a human body and the head of a jackal. This god was believed to be responsible for the process of embalming, which preserved the bodies of the dead. Anubis often appears in wall paintings and sculptures found in burial places. Here he is shown embalming the body of an Egyptian king.

Relatives and Namesakes

Wolves, foxes and other members of the dog family have taken millions of years to evolve (develop). Scientists can trace their history through bones and other fossils preserved in the Earth from ancient times. Somewhere around 65 million years ago, a family of tree-dwelling mammals called miacids developed. These carnivorous mammals tore the flesh from their prey using jagged carnassial teeth similar to those of modern dogs and wolves. Later, around 30 million years ago, one branch of the miacid family evolved into fast-running, mongoose-like creatures called cynodictis. In turn, cynodictis and relatives such as hesperocyon developed into the first distinctively wolf-like creatures. From such ancestors, modern canids evolved around 300,000 years ago.

▲ ANCIENT ANCESTOR

Hesperocyon was the prehistoric ancestor of wolves and other carnivores. It had a long, dog-like snout and sharp carnassial teeth. Over millions of years, hesperocyons had evolved from earlier tree-dwelling creatures, called miacids. Miacids gradually evolved strong legs and feet to make them fast runners.

◄ DIRE WOLVES

The long-extinct dire wolf was an ancient relative of the modern wolf. Remains of these prehistoric creatures have been found in fossil pits in California. Dire wolves lived on Earth about two million years ago. They were fierce predators, much bigger than today's wolves, that preyed on large camelids (camels) and American rhinos (both now extinct) and (the now rare) bison.

◄ WOLF-DOG HYBRID

A wolf-dog skirts farmland in Italy. This animal is the offspring of a gray wolf and a German shepherd dog. Coy-wolves, red wolves and coy-dogs are other hybrids that resulted from interbreeding between coyotes, wolves and domestic dogs. These animals may resemble domestic dogs, but they cannot usually be tamed.

TASMANIAN WOLVES ►

This engraving of the 1800s shows two thylacines, or Tasmanian wolves. As the name suggests, these creatures lived on the island of Tasmania, off Australia. With their long snouts and strong legs, thylacines looked a lot like wild dogs and barked like dogs, too. However, they were marsupials, a group of mammals that carries its young in pouches. Their natural prey was kangaroos and wallabies, but when they started to take sheep farmers hunted them to extinction.

Did you know? Dogs have been domesticated for at least 12,000 years.

Tasmanian wolf
(Thylacinus cynocephalus)

▲ SCAVENGERS AT WORK

Hyenas gather at a Kenyan water hole to finish off a buffalo killed by lions. Hyenas look like African hunting dogs, but are from the Hyaenidae family. They can crunch through the toughest bones with their powerful jaws and strong, sharp teeth.

▲ DESCENDED FROM ONE ANCESTOR

All domestic dogs are descended from the wolf. Human and dog came together thousands of years ago for mutual benefit. By Roman times, around 500 B.C., many of the breeds we know today had already developed.

113

Fact or Fiction?

Myths, fairy tales and even modern movies depict wolves as bold, wicked hunters that prey on humans, especially young children. In fact, there have been very few confirmed accounts of wolves attacking people, and none in North America, one of the animal's main strongholds. Wolves were more likely to have been a menace in Europe before guns were invented. Then, they probably had little fear of humans and may have prowled close to villages in the hope of stealing sheep and other domestic beasts. Wolves may have acquired their reputation as man-eaters by scavenging meat from dead bodies on battlefields. In modern times, the rare attacks on people have probably been made by wolves suffering from rabies, a disease that makes animals behave abnormally.

▲ **TALL TALE**
In 1901, a pack of wolves was reported to have attacked and eaten a group of five Romanian soldiers. Suspiciously, no trace of the men was left except their blood-stained weapons. This event is hard to believe, since even starving wolves would be unlikely to attack a band of well-armed men.

◄ **ALWAYS ALERT**
A modern-day shepherd tends his flock in the remote Spanish mountains. He has only his dogs and a stout stick to scare away any wolves that threaten his flock. An experienced shepherd, however, knows that wolves are easily frightened.

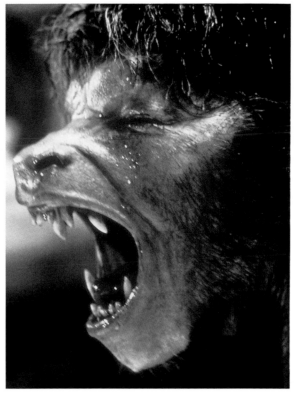

▲ WOLF MAGIC

Native Americans thought of wolves as magical creatures. This shaman (medicine man) is dressed in a wolf skin to take on the creature's power. He calls upon the wolf spirit to give his patient the strength to recover from illness.

▲ HOWLING AT THE MOON

Werewolves are a popular subject of horror movies. In folk tales, these are humans who turn into wolves when there is a full moon. They can only be killed by a silver bullet.

▲ WOLVES BLAMED FOR ATTACK

In 1907, wolves were said to have attacked a group of Hungarian gypsies. There was no real proof, however, and the attack may have been carried out by a gang of robbers.

◀ SLY OLD FOX

In this scene from one of Aesop's *Fables*, a clever vixen (female fox) tries to outwit a rooster crowing at dawn. She says to the rooster that she would like to embrace the owner of such a fine voice. Wolves and foxes are portrayed as villains in many folk tales and legends. They are frequently described as sly and cunning, terms that show them in a negative light.

Natural Enemies

Wolves and wild dogs may be powerful predators, but they face many threats in the wild. Their natural enemies include the largest creatures that they hunt, such as moose, bison and musk oxen. The sharp hooves and horns of these animals can fatally wound a predator. One careless slip, and a wolf may be gored or trampled to death. Wolves and wild dogs are also threatened when their habitats are disturbed or destroyed. In many areas, the territories where wild dogs can roam free are getting smaller and smaller. Land is needed for crops or to graze herds of sheep and cattle. Forests are cut down for timber or to make way for new roads and towns. The survival of wolves and wild dogs is also threatened by deadly diseases such as distemper, anthrax and rabies.

▲ HUNTING THE HUNTERS
A lioness has killed an African hunting dog. Groups of lions are known to stalk and ambush hunting dogs while they feed on a kill, or drink at water holes. Hyenas and jackals also prey on hunting dogs. They sneak up to the den and steal young pups if the adult dogs are not keeping a careful watch.

▼ DEFENSE TACTICS
On the Arctic tundra, large, shaggy musk oxen form a defensive ring around their young. Their long, fierce horns face outward, keeping young and weak members of the herd safe from wolves.

◄ DANGEROUS TARGET

A moose browses among the tall lakeside shrubs in Wyoming. Moose are powerful beasts. An adult male stands 6 ft tall at the shoulder and weighs as much as ten wolves. Its antlers and hooves can inflict great damage. A moose can crack a wolf's skull with one mighty kick, or gore it with its antlers and toss it high in the air. Wolves must be very wary when hunting such dangerous prey.

DINGOES KEEP OUT ►

A dingo attacks a sheep, snapping at its hindquarters. Farmers have built a great fence across 3,500 mi. of southeastern Australia to keep dingoes out of sheep country. Any dog caught inside the fence is shot.

▲ DEADLY RABIES

A black-backed jackal lies dying of rabies. Rabies is a fatal disease that attacks the brain and nervous system. It is passed on by saliva from an infected bite. Wild dogs have been wiped out in many areas to prevent rabies spreading to humans, even though a vaccine is available.

▲ KEEP OFF THE ROAD

African hunting dogs roam along a newly built road that cuts across their territory in the bush. They are scavenging for road-kills, but may well become victims themselves. The rapid human development of the dogs' territory threatens their way of life and very survival.

119

Wild Dogs and People

Wherever wolves and wild dogs come into contact with people, the animals are regarded as dangerous pests that will—given the chance— kill livestock. They are poisoned, trapped and shot, not only for their skins, but for sport. Wolves were once the most widespread carnivores in the northern hemisphere. Now they survive in a much reduced area, often in small, scattered groups. Several species are endangered, including the Simien wolf, the red wolf and the African hunting dog. Much of the land where these animals once lived is now being farmed. Dholes and bush dogs have also become very rare as their forest habitat is destroyed. Some species, such as the Falkland Island wolf, a kind of fox, are already extinct.

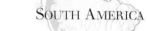

NORTH AMERICA

SOUTH AMERICA

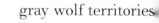

gray wolf territories

▲ **WOLF HUNT**

In the Middle Ages domestic dogs were often used to kill wolves, as this Dutch engraving of 1880 shows. The last wolves were wiped out in England by 1500 and in Ireland by 1800.

Tame Wolf
This book is a first edition of the popular novel White Fang *by American writer Jack London. Set in northern Canada, it describes how a wolf, named White Fang, is tamed and becomes a pet. In general it is not against the law to keep a wolf as a pet, but countries with restrictions require owners to have a special permit. The* Call of the Wild *by the same author describes how a pet dog joins a wolf pack and becomes wild.*

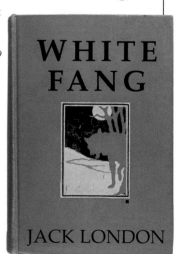

WHITE FANG

JACK LONDON

◀ NOWHERE TO RUN

A hunter in Colorado shoulders a coyote he has shot. In country areas, farmers shoot or poison coyotes because they steal sheep and other livestock and spread disease. Elsewhere, when coyotes and other wild dogs enter towns to scrounge scraps, they risk being shot as pests.

▲ WOLF TERRITORY

Gray wolves once had the greatest range of any wild land mammal. In the past, wolves were once common all across North America, throughout Europe, the Middle East and most of Asia. Their present range shows they have been exterminated in most of Mexico and the United States, in almost all of western Europe and over much of Asia.

▼ AN UNKIND LUXURY

Fox fur was very fashionable in the early 1900s, mainly for coats and for trimming garments. The fox fur stole (scarf) shown here uses the pelt (fur and skin) of an entire animal. In the past, furs were worn mainly to keep warm in winter. Today, however, man-made fabrics are as warm as fur, making it unnecessary and cruel to kill these animals for their pelts.

▲ UNDER THREAT

A Simien wolf howls high in the Ethiopian mountains. As the human population grows, more land is farmed and the animal's range is restricted. Simien wolves are shot for fur and killed by farmers as pests. There may be only 500 Simien wolves left in the wild.

121

Conservation

▲ SUCCESS STORY
Conservationists release a red wolf that was bred in captivity into a reserve in North Carolina. Red wolves were once found throughout the southeastern United States. They nearly became extinct, but breeding programs have saved the species.

In many parts of the world, efforts are being made to save threatened wolves and wild dogs. Gray wolves have recently been reintroduced into areas where they had died out. Conservationists working to protect wolves face opposition from local farmers who fear that wolves will kill their livestock. In some preserves, wolves and wild dogs have begun to be promoted as tourist attractions. This helps people to learn about these animals and the entrance fees help to finance conservation work. Today, wolves and their relatives are gradually losing their bad image. More and more people are appreciating their admirable qualities—intelligence, loyalty and strong family ties. In the wild, these predators actually help to improve stocks of prey animals. By hunting mostly weak or sickly individuals, they help to ensure the survival of the fittest.

◀ RADIO TRACKING
A red wolf has been fitted with a radio collar. The collar allows scientists to track the animal as it roams the wilds. Radio tracking helps to provide scientists with valuable information about the wolf's habits and range. Increasing such knowledge also helps conservationists with their work.

▲ STAR OF THE SHOW

Tourists on safari photograph African hunting dogs in a preserve. In recent years, such tourist attractions have earned much needed cash for remote villages. The money helps to persuade local people not to hunt the dogs, but to see them as a valuable asset instead.

▲ HELPING TO KEEP THE BALANCE

A pack of wolves feeds on a deer carcass. By targeting old and sick animals, the wolves actually help the rest of the herd to survive. They may be removing a deer whose sickness could infect others in the herd, or an old animal whose share of food could be better used to rear healthy young.

▼ SOUND OF THE WILD

For many people, the wolf is a symbol of the wilderness. Now in some countries, wolves are becoming a tourist attraction. At some centers, members of the public can even walk alongside tame wolves, petting them if they wish, accompanied, of course, by expert handlers.

▲ WOLF RESEARCH

Scientists check the teeth of a drugged Arctic wolf. Researchers sometimes capture the same wolves several times over the course of a number of years to study their life histories. This work helps to provide evidence of the strong family ties and keen intelligence of the wolf.

GLOSSARY

adapt
When an animal or group of animals changes—physically or in behavior—in order to survive in new conditions.

alpha pair
The top male and female in a wolf pack. Only this strong, healthy pair of animals breeds.

altitude
The height of a place given in feet or meters above sea level.

ambush
When an animal hides, waiting for prey to walk past, and pounces on it in a surprise attack.

binocular vision
The ability to see things with both eyes at the same time.

breed
A sub-group of animals within a species, with definite characteristics, such as coloring, body shape and coat markings.

camouflage
Colors or patterns that allow an animal to blend in with its surroundings to avoid detection.

canid
A member of the dog family, such as wolves, jackals, and foxes.

canines
The sharp, pointed teeth that dogs and cats use for killing prey.

carnassials
The strong, shearing teeth at the back of a cat's or dog's mouth.

carnivore
An animal that feeds mainly on the flesh of other animals.

carrion
The body of a dead animal.

classification
Arranging animals according to their similarities and differences in order to study how they may be related.

conservationist
A person who works to protect the Earth's natural resources.

cub
A young wolf or dog, or big cat.

den
The home of an animal such as a wolf or lion. A den may be an underground burrow or a cave, or simply a nest in the long grass.

dew claw
The digit (toe) on a cat's front foot that is held off the ground to keep it sharp. It is used to knock down and hold on to prey. In a wolf it is high on the foreleg.

digestion
The process by which food is broken down so that it can be absorbed by the body.

domesticated
Animals that have been tamed by people, such as the domestic cat.

dominance
A system between social animals, such as lions or wolves, in which one or a few animals rule the group. The rulers have first choice over more junior members.

Equator
An imaginary line running around the centre of the Earth, separating north and south.

esophagus
Part of the gut that transports food from the mouth to the stomach.

evolve
When a species of animals or plants changes gradually over time, to become better suited to the conditions in which it lives.

extinct
When a whole species or larger group of animals or plants has disappeared, dying out completely.

fossil
The remains of plants or animals that have turned to stone over thousands or millions of years.

gland
An organ in the body that produces chemicals for a particular use.

habitat
A type of place where certain animals and plants live, such as a tropical rainforest, the savanna, or a desert.

herbivore
A kind of animal that eats plants.

hierarchy
A strict social order within a group of animals.

hybrid
The offspring of two animals from different species or subspecies.

incisors
The front teeth, which cats and dogs use for cutting up meat.

insulation
A covering, like a cat's fur coat, that does not allow too much heat in or out of the body.

intestine
Part of the gut of an animal specialized to digest food.

jungle
The dense undergrowth found in a rainforest.

kidney
An organ of the body that filters blood to remove waste products, called urine.

litter
A group of young animals born to a mother at one time.

liver
An organ that processes food from the digestive system (gut). One of the liver's main tasks is to remove any poisons from the blood.

lungs
An organ of the body that takes in oxygen from the air.

mammal
A warm-blooded animal that has an internal skeleton, usually hair or fur on its body, and mammary glands that produce milk to feed its babies.

mangrove
Tree that grows in muddy swamps near the sea.

mating
The pairing up of a male and female to produce young. During mating, the fertilization (joining together) of a male sperm and a female egg takes place, which starts a new life.

membrane
A thin layer of skin that separates one area from another.

milk teeth
A young animal's first teeth, which are replaced by permanent teeth.

molt
To shed fur or feathers.

muzzle
The jaws and nose of an animal such as a wolf.

nerves
Fibres that carry electrical impulses to and from the brain.

nocturnal
Describes an animal that rests by day and is active at night.

pack
The name given to a group of wolves or wild dogs that live and hunt together.

poaching
Capturing and/or killing animals illegally and selling their body parts for commercial gain.

predator
An animal that catches and kills other animals (prey) for its food.

prey
An animal that is hunted for food by another animal (predator).

rainforest
A tropical forest where it is hot and wet all year.

range
The area in which an animal species lives.

regurgitate
When an animal brings up half digested swallowed food to feed its young.

rendezvous
A meeting place that lies in the heart of a wolf pack's territory. This is a safe place where wolves gather and cubs play.

125

rodent
An animal with chisel-shaped front teeth used for gnawing.

savanna
Hot, open grasslands found in tropical regions, with a few scattered trees.

scavenger
An animal that feeds on the remains of other animals' meals, or on animals that died naturally.

scent-mark
To mark the edge of a territory by spraying urine. The scent lingers for several days after the animal has moved on.

skeleton
The bony framework of an animal's body.

social animal
An animal that lives in a large group, usually with others of its own kind.

species
All living things are grouped into species. Animals of the same species are similar to each other and can breed with each other. They produce young that in turn can breed together. Each species is given a unique name.

stalk
To follow prey quietly and carefully so that a predator is within striking distance.

submissive
When a junior animal gives way to a more powerful animal.

subspecies
A species is sometimes divided into smaller groups called subspecies, which are sufficiently distinct to have their own group.

sweat glands
Small organs beneath an animal's skin that produce sweat. Sweat helps to keep the body cool.

taste buds
Tiny bumps on an animal's tongue, which have nerve endings that pick up taste signals.

territory
An area in which an animal or group of animals live. Many animals use scent to mark the borders of their territories to keep other animals of the same species out.

trachea
The windpipe running from the nose and mouth used to transport air to the lungs.

track
To follow the scent of another animal, usually for prey.

tropics
Warm, wet regions of the Earth that lie close to the Equator.

tundra
The cold, treeless lowlands of the far north. Summers are very short here. During the winter the sun hardly rises at all and it is dark for most of the day.

turbinates
Tubes of very thin bones in the roof of a wolf's snout. These are connected to a nerve network that sends signals to the brain.

vein
A blood vessel that carries blood back toward the heart.

warm-blooded
An animal that is able to keep its body temperature at the same level all the time.

wean
When a young animal moves from drinking only its mother's milk to a diet of solid food.

whiskers
Long, stiff hairs on a animal's face with sensitive nerve endings at their roots.

INDEX

A

African hunting dog 70–1, 75, 81, 82–3, 87, 91, 93, 96–8, 101, 102, 109, 119, 123

alpha pair 88–9, 91, 98–9

Andean mountain cat 48

Arctic fox 103, 104, 114

Arctic wolf 68, 81, 104, 123

B

balance 8–9, 11, 22, 25

bat-eared fox 77

beta pair 88

black-backed jackal 69, 80, 93, 108, 119

bobcat 23, 48–9

body language 8, 19, 26–7, 88–9

bones 12–13, 74–5, 112

breeding 40–1, 86–8, 98–101, 108, 110–11

bush dog 70, 79, 94, 120

C

camouflage 20–1, 32, 43, 49, 54, 80–1, 105, 108, 114–15

canids 66–7, 71, 112

carnivores 8, 28–9, 66–7, 92–3, 96, 101, 102

cheetah 10, 12, 14–15, 20, 21, 24–5, 27, 28–31, 34–5, 41, 44, 47, 54–7

CITES convention 62, 79

claws 8, 10, 14–15, 24, 79

climbing 12, 14, 22, 33, 48–50

clouded leopard 10, 50

colpeo fox 115

communication 8, 18–19, 26–7, 52, 82–5, 88–9, 90–1, 102

conservation 59–60, 62–3, 122–3

Coppers 92, 112, 120

courtship 27, 38–9, 53, 74, 78, 92–3

coy-dog 113

coy-wolf 113

coyote 66, 68, 69, 78, 82, 86–7, 92, 95, 108–11, 121

crab-eating fox 115

cubs and pups 27, 34–7, 40–5, 53, 66, 86–7, 90, 98–103, 104, 209

D

dens and burrows 40–1, 66, 98–9, 100–1, 108

desert dwellers 56–7, 108

dew claws 14, 25, 78

dhole 70, 82, 87, 91, 93, 94–5, 120

digestive system 15, 28, 76

dingo 68–9, 79, 80, 95, 99, 108, 119

dire wolf 112

diseases 116, 118–19

domestic cat 8, 10

domestic dog 69, 72–3, 113, 120

drinking 18, 34, 53, 55–6, 84, 86, 108

E

ears 9, 17, 26–7, 66, 67, 82, 108

Egypt, ancient 57, 60, 63, 109

endangered species 59–60, 62–3, 120–3

extinct species 68, 112–13, 120, 122–3

eyes 8–9, 13, 16–17, 67, 83, 100

F

Falkland Island dog 120

fennec fox 114

feral dog 109

fighting 26, 37–8, 52

flehmen 19

food 8, 12, 15, 18, 28–31, 41, 92–3

fossils 112

fox 66, 74–5, 79, 86, 91, 108, 114–15, 117, 121

fur 8–9, 20–1, 23, 43, 46, 66–7, 80–1, 85, 104–5, 114, 121

   killing for 47, 60–1, 62

G

golden jackal 69, 80

gray fox 79

gray wolf 68, 78, 81, 88–9, 93, 101, 105, 121, 122

greyhound 73

grooming 9, 19, 35, 42, 85

guard hairs 20, 80

H

hearing 8–9, 16–17, 26, 66, 67, 82

hesperocyon 112

hissing 26, 40

howling 82, 91, 98, 110, 117

humans

  and cats 46–7, 58–61, 62–3

  and dogs 69, 70, 72–3, 104, 105, 116–17, 120–3

hunting 8–9, 14–17, 22–5, 28–31, 32, 42–5, 49, 63, 66–7, 68, 74–5, 76, 79, 82–3, 92–7, 118–19

husky 105

hybrids 68, 113

hyoid bone 10

I

intelligence 66, 76, 122

intestines 15, 76

J

jackal 66–7, 68–9, 80, 86, 109, 118

Jacobson's organ 19

jaguar 11, 21–2, 28–9, 50–1, 54, 56, 59

jaws 13, 66, 77, 84

K

keratin 15

killing prey 25, 28, 30–1, 43–4, 52, 92–5, 96–7

legs 22, 66, 74–5, 78–9

leopard 10–12, 16, 18, 21, 22, 26, 28, 32–3, 38, 44, 47–8, 50–1, 54–8, 61, 62

lion 8–10, 13–15, 17, 19, 22–3, 26–31, 34–9, 41–3, 45–7, 54–6, 58, 62

litters 40–3, 66

lone wolf 89

lynx 17, 48–9

M

mammal 8, 66, 100–1

mane 10, 36, 41, 81

maned wolf 70–1, 74, 79, 81, 86–7, 93, 94, 98, 103, 108–9

margay 50–1

mating 19, 27, 32, 34, 36, 38–9, 53, 98–9

Mexican wolf 68

miacid 112

milk 41, 66, 100–1, 102

mountain cat 48

mountain dwellers 48–9

movement 8, 22–3, 78–9

muscles 8, 12, 14–15, 42, 76–7, 78

muzzle 66, 85

N

Native Americans 75, 104, 117

nictitating membrane 83

nocturnal species 63, 94

nose 14, 18, 24, 66, 84, 85

O

ocelot 50

P

pack 67, 84, 86–9, 90–1, 94–7, 98, 102–3,109

panther 11, 21, 51

paws 8–9, 13–15, 22–4, 67, 78–9, 85

play 37, 42–4, 83, 85, 102–3

predators 40–1, 43, 44–7, 118–21

prey 14–17, 24–5, 29–31, 33, 43–4, 58–9, 92–7

prides 10, 31, 34–7, 45, 47

puma 10, 17, 21, 34, 41, 48–9

R

rabies 116, 118–19

raccoon dog 70–1, 80, 86, 92, 94

red fox 115

red wolf 68, 113, 120, 122

rendezvous 90, 102

roaring 26, 52

running 22–5, 66, 74–5, 76, 78–9

S

sand cat 56–7

scent glands 24–7, 84

scent-marking 26–7, 35, 42, 90, 91

scratching 26–7, 45

senses 16–17, 66–7, 82–5, 90–1, 94

serval 54–5

side-striped jackal 69, 80

sight 8–9, 13, 16–17, 54, 82–3

Simien wolf 68, 101, 120, 121

skeleton 12–13, 74–5

smell, sense of 26, 35, 38, 42, 73, 84–5, 94

snow leopard 10–11, 19, 21, 34, 40, 48–9

social behavior 10, 29–31, 34–7, 52, 66–7, 74–9, 102–3, 110–11, 122

spine 12–13, 22, 24, 74

steppe wolf 68, 103

T

tail 8–9, 11, 19, 22, 25–6, 49, 66–7, 74–5, 84

tapetum lucidum 16–17

taste, sense of 18–19, 84

tear stripes 20

teeth 8, 12–13, 43, 45, 52, 66, 74, 76–7

temperature 76, 98–9

territorial behavior 34–6, 45, 52, 90–1, 104, 110

tiger 8, 10–12, 15, 18–23, 27, 39–40, 50–3, 58–61, 63

Tippu's Tiger 59

tongue 18–19, 42, 84–5

touch, sense of 16, 18–19, 84–5

tracking 73, 84–5, 94

W

werewolf 117

whiskers 8, 18–19

PICTURE CREDITS

ABPL: 11tl, 21cbl & cbr, 27c, /Daryl Balfour: 47t, /Peter Chadwick: 23t, /Nigel Dennis: 10b, 22t, 24t, 57t, /Clem Haagner: 8–9c, 14b, 30t, 45t, 55cr, 56b, /Dave Hamman: 29tr, 55t, /Roger de la Harpe: 21ctl, /Lex Hes: 32t & b, /Gerald Hinde: 16b, 33t, 37tl, /Luke Hunter: 36–7c, 43tl, 47b, /Beverly Joubert: 28c, 42t, 45c, /Peter Lillie: 25t, 28b, /Anup Shah: 24c, 44b, 45b, /Giselle Wurfsohn: 61tl. Bryan and Cherry Alexander Photography: 85tr, 88br, 89tl, 90t, 99br, 105c, 123cr. Anness/Jane Burton: 63t. Ardea London/Chris Martin Bahr: 73cl, /Liz Bonford 88bl, /John Daniels: 72b & 73tl, /Jean Paul Ferrero: 80b, 95tl, 119c, /François Gohier: 108t, /M. Krishnan: 109tl, /Stefan Meyers: 106b. The Art Archive/George Catlin: 117tl. BBC Natural History Unit/ Christopher Becker: 91tr, /R Couper Johnston: 71b, /Richard Du Toit: 81tr, 97b, /Jeff Foot: 68tr, /Louis Gagnon: 67cr, /C Hamilton James: 68b, 101br, /Andrew Harrington: 91tl, /Tony Heald: 71c, /Simon King: 98t, 99bl, 108br, /Lockwood & Dattatri: 87tl, 95br, /Ron O'Connor: 119br, /Pete Oxford: 69cr, 82bl, 109tr, /Françoise Savigny: 86tr, /Keith Scholes: 25b, 75br, /Vadim Sidorovich: 92t, /Lynn Stone: 10c, 105b, 123tr, /Tom Vezo: 17tl, 103, 81br, 125bl, /Bernard Walton: 113t. Bridgeman Art Library: 28t, 35tr, 57br, 60b, 94t, 109br. Bruce Coleman Collection/Atlantide: 116b, /Erwin & Peggy Bauer: 23b, 30bl, 31b, 41c, 50b, 102t, 103b, 113bl, /Alain Compost: 21t, 51tl & cl, /Gerald Cubitt: 62bl, /Bruce Davidson: 96t & b, 97cl, /Peter Evans: 37b, /Jeff Foot: 119t, /Christer Fredriksson: 29b, /Paul van Gaalen: 17tr, /HPH Photography: 13bl, /Leonard Lee Rue: 19t, 31c, /Joe McDonald: 31t, 35br, 38b, 55b, /Antonio Manzanares: 29tl, /Rita Meyer: 19b, 108bl, /Dieter & Mary Plage: 41br, 49c, /Michael Price: 63c, / Hans Reinhard: 23c, 48b, 67br, 77br, /John Shaw: 9b, 34b, /Kim Taylor: 13t, /Norman Tomalin: 26t, 37tr, /Staffan Widstrand: 104b, /Rod Williams: 39b, 49b, 51tr, 57c, 81tl, 103cl, /Gunter Ziesler: 30br, 48t. C M Dixon: 58t, 59t, 62t. Mary Evans Picture Library: 55cl, 58b, 61tr, 103cr, 116t, 117bl, 120bl, 120br. FLPA: 47cl, /E & D Hosking: 65b, /Leonard Lee Rue: 54b, /Mark Newman: 44t, /Philip Perry: 18t, 27tr, 39t, 56t, 57bl, /Fritz Pölking: 22b, 24b, 25c, /Terry Whittaker: 9tl, 15t, 17b, 21b, 27b, 40t, 53t & b, /E Woods: 41bl. Gettyone Stone Images /Art Wolf: 89tr, /Rosemary Calvert: 83c, /Kathy Bushue: 103tl, 104cr. Grant Museum/A Lister: 13br. Griffith Institute, Ashmolean Museum: 60t. Michael Holford: 14t, /Niall McInerney: 61br. The Kobal Collection: 117tr. Natural History Museum: 62. Natural Science Photos/

D Allen Photography: 10t, 26b, 33c, 46t, 47cr, 54t, /Ken Cole: 11c, 12b, 52t, /Carlo Dani & Ingrid Jeske: 11b, 41t, 63t, /Lex Hes: 21b, 34–5t, /C Jones: 38t, /David Lawson: 34c, /Michael Kock: 61bl, /M W Powles: 35bl, /Keren Su: 52br, /John Warden: 40b, 46b, 49t. NHPA/K. Ghani: 93t, /Martin Harvey: 59br, 69tr, /Rich Kirchner: 87c, 98b, /T Kitchin & V Hurst: 79br, 95bl, 111c & b, /Stephen Krasemann: 122t, 123bl, 125br, /Gerard Lacz: 81c, /Yves Lanceau: 16t, /Christophe Ratier: 62br, /Andy Rouse: 50t, 88tl, 101tl, /Jany Sauvanet: 79c, 107cl, 115tr & b, /Mirko Stelzner: 107t. Oxford Scientific Films/Anthony Bannister: 93cr, /Bob Bennett: 110b, /Joel Bennett: 118b, /Rafi Ben-Shahar: 118t, 123tl, /Matthias Breiter: 122b, /Alan & Sandy Carey: 87tl, /David Cayless: 97t, cr & b, /Daniel J Cox: 75cr, 78tl, 78bl, 82tl, 85bl, 89b, 99cr, 100t, 111cl, 125t, 126t & b, /Richard Day: 92b, /Nick Gordon: 70t, 124bl, /Mike Hill: 106t, /Lon E Lauber: 84t, 85c, 95bl, 111tr, 124cr, /Michael Leach: 93cl, /Matthews/Purdy: 101bl, /Victoria McCormick: 82br, /Joe McDonald: 109bl, /Owen Newman: 121cr, /Stan Osolinski: 77tr, /Richard Packwood: 102b, /Charles Palek: 75tr, /Krupaker Senani: 91c, /Michael Sewell: 93b, /Vivek Sinha: 107cr, /Claude Steelman: 121t, /M & C Tibbles: 100b, /Steve Turner: 80t,119bl, /Tom Ulrich: 105tr, /Anna Walsh: 121bl, /Peter Weiman: 91b, /Colin Willcock: 105tl, /Konrad Wothe: 84br, 99t, /Villarosa/ Overseas: 107b. Papilio Photographic: 8t, 11tr, 19c, 20t, 21ctr, 27tl, 51bl, 52bl, 110t. Planet Earth Pictures: 39c, 43b, 51br, /Geoff Johnson: 18b, /Ken Lucas: 77tl, /Nicholas Parfitt: 36r, /Bryan Parsley: 53c, /Mark Petersen: 33b, /Anup Shah: 43tr, /Manoj Shah: 36t, 42bl & br; Tony Stone: 8b. Science Photo Library /George Bernard: 113c, 124t. Still Pictures/Klein Hubert: 69cl, 114bl & br, /John Newby: 114t. Visual Arts Library: 9tr. Warren Photographic /Jane Burton: 83tl. Werner Forman Archive: 59bl.